The Broadview Book of

Sports Anecdotes

THE BROADVIEW BOOK OF
SPORTS
ANECDOTES

edited by
Brendan Connor

broadview press

Canadian Cataloguing in Publication Data

The Broadview Book of sports anecdotes

ISBN 0-921149-43-3

1. Sports - Anecdotes. 2. Sports - Humor.
I. Connor, Brendan. II. Title: Sports anecdotes.

GV707.B76 1989   796'.0207   C89-095125-X

Broadview Press   in the US: Broadview Press
PO Box 1243   421 Center St.
Peterborough, Canada K9J 7H5   Lewiston, NY 14092

Printed and bound in Canada

To my parents, Michael and Lynn Connor,
a couple of great sports whom I love dearly.

Preface

Sport is one area where no participant is worried about another's race, religion or wealth, and where the only concern is "Have you come to play?"

Henry Roxborough

For me, sports is a world full of fascinating stories about people. Scores and statistics you can get anywhere the day after the game. Certainly, sports achievement or failure must be measured on the surface in terms of wins, losses, times, distances, and totals; more interesting to me, though, are the human stories behind that achievement or failure.

There has been some great prose written by some amazingly talented people about some epic events in sports and, by extension, in life. To read a Scott Young or a Jim Coleman writing passionately about the sports they love is literature and is to be savoured. To read a personal narrative from an NFL war-horse like Ken Stabler, or to see NHL stars from the perspective of a veteran referee like Bruce Hood is fascinating. Great stories are out in the sports world like pebbles on a beach. All we have to do is pick them up. I've picked up a few pebbles for you and collected them in this book.

I hope you enjoy them.

Brendan Connor
Kingston, July 1989

Acknowledgements

Several people were extremely supportive in the concept and compilation of this book. I must thank the publisher, Don LePan, for his patience and encouragement and for coming to me with the idea. My gratitude goes as well to the staff at Broadview Press; to Kari for the marshalling of all my material and for working tirelessly on the copyright matters; to Kim and Fred and Jill for being pleasant to me on the phone when I called with queries; to the proofreaders and typesetters as well... thank you.

To my colleagues at CBC and in the other media, thanks for putting up with my prattle about this project.

And to my wife, Bev, thanks most of all. Your humour, affection and support are what keep the fires of ambition burning in me.

You know my love.

Brendan

1

Soccer
The World's Most Popular Sport

At its best, it's a stately old game, steeped in tradition and fanned by the flames of patriotic passion. At its worst, it's a game where crowd mentality and anonymity wreak havoc and tarnish the sport.

Soccer is the number one sport in the world.

It is a game played in more than 140 nations under uniform rules, and in most countries, particularly in Europe and South America, it is the predominating sport, enlisting a large number of participants and commanding a greater popular appeal than any other single sport. The World Cup, an international soccer summit held every four years, attracts more watchers, in person and on television, than any other sporting event on the planet.

Soccer furnishes, to the highest degree, the principles of open play, swift action, skill, individual effort, team strategy, discipline, excitement and thrills.

At the recreational level, it has provided millions with a spirited pastime. At the professional level, it has provided skilled players with an avenue out of poverty. It has also driven fans to bizarre heights of nationalistic fervor, from the flag-waving delirium of Italian fans everywhere in 1982 when that country won the World Cup to the horrors of hooliganism and death at soccer matches in Britain, Europe and South America.

Did you know the beginnings of the game date back to the Roman occupation of ancient Britain?

Actually, it's real origin is so obscure that one might be forgiven for suggesting that maybe Adam kicked an apple around the Garden of Eden to the amusement of Eve. First claim on the game comes from the Romans, who had a game in which the "follis," a large inflated ball, was used. The follis, however, was undoubtedly a handball, and the game was probably the same as the "balown ball" of the Middle Ages, in which an inflated ball was knocked in the air and kept there as long as possible. The follis was also the early model for a football.

It was in Chester, England, centuries ago, that the people played football on Shrove Tuesdays. Contemporary historians suggest it was the head of a Dane who had been captured and slain that was used for a ball and kicked about for sport.

Derby, England claims that game was born there, also on a Shrove Tuesday, to celebrate a victory by a troop of British warriors in the year 217 A.D.

In records from the year 1186, mentions are made of "London schoolboys annually upon Shrove Tuesdays going to the fields to play at the well-known game of ball."

In the 14th century, the game appears to have drawn the ire of the authorities. On April 13, 1314, Edward II issued a proclamation forbidding the game as leading to a breach of the peace "forasmuch as there is great noise in the city caused by hustling over large balls from which many evils might arise. We commend and forbid, on behalf of the king, on pain of imprisonment, such game to be used in the city in the future."

In 1349, football is mentioned in a statute of Edward III, who objected to the game as tending to discourage the practice of archery, upon which the military strength of the country depended. In 1459, James III decreed that "footballe and golfe be utterly cryed down and not to be used."

In 1779, for playing football on a Sunday, one John Wonkell was sent to prison for a week and ordered to do penance in the church.

In those days games lasted many hours and the goals were usually at opposite ends of the hamlets or towns. It was lawful to kick an opponent in the shins or to trip him; in fact, anything went in order to get or keep the ball away from an opposing player.

Not all of this is simply lore. Sufficient evidence to the antiquity of the sport is offered in this passage from Act II of Shakespeare's "Comedy of Errors."

"Am I so round with you as you with me
That like a football you do spurn me thus?
You spurn me hence and he will spurn me hither;
If I last in this service you must case me in leather."

Although it may be true that football, or soccer, in those days found
no place in the annals of knight errantry, nevertheless it found a warm
spot in the hearts of the common people. Though prohibited by kings
and queens, it defied and survived the law; fulminated against by
churchmen, it survived their dogmatic ranting; attacked by the pens of
writers, it has outlived them all, for it is now played under the same rules
all over the civilized world.

2

Arthur Irwin
HANDYman

A Canadian, playing for a major league baseball team in Providence,
Rhode Island in 1883 was responsible for the introduction of the glove
to baseball.

Arthur Irwin of Toronto had broken the third and fourth fingers of his
left hand while playing in a game. In those days teams only carried ten
or eleven players and each man was pretty much his own substitute, playing as long as was physically possible. Determined to remain in the
Providence lineup, Irwin visited a glove-maker in the city who took a
buckskin driving glove and added some padding. He then sewed together
the third and fourth fingers and presented the finished product to the
Providence shortstop.

When Irwin came out on the field the next day he fully expected to
be ridiculed by players and fans alike, since a glove was unheard of for
a baseball player. Players were considered too manly to wear any
protective equipment.

To his amazement, Irwin was not ridiculed and completed the game without a problem. Not long afterward, another ballplayer who had no injury, John Montgomery Ward, took a liking to Irwin's idea and ordered a glove made. Nobody complained and soon gloves were being ordered by hundreds of enthusiastic ballplayers.

3

The 1908 Olympics
Helped Across the Line

One of the most remarkable episodes in Olympic history was reported for the New York Herald Tribune *by Sir Arthur Conan Doyle:*

After the start of the Marathon Race from Windsor, the leaders were announced, and then a man in a white uniform would parade around the arena, bearing a signboard, on which appeared the names of the British runners who were in the van.

At the first mile, two Britons were announced in the lead and the crowd was enthusiastic; at four miles, three Britishers still led; at the ninth, one had been displaced by the South African, Hefferon, and the same men were announced at eighteen miles.

At the nineteenth mile, a feeling of doubt seemed for the first time to strike the spectators when an Italian was announced to be one of the three in the lead. At the twentieth mile, no Englishman was announced. He had given place to number 26, but by the ghost of British fair play this could not be, and they looked at their programs, rubbed their eyes. "Ah! Hayes, a bloody Yankee."

At three minutes before five o'clock, the course inside the Stadium was cleared. From that time, the vast gathering waited almost breathless. It seemed as if absolute silence had fallen. Then came the announcement that Hefferon of South Africa and Dorando of Italy were leading.

With true British impartiality, the name of Hayes was left out. The crowd at the back of the north end of the stand rose and scanned the road to Windsor. At twenty-four miles, the same announcement was made and bombs were set off.

"What has become of Hayes?" Americans anxiously inquired of each other. To relieve the tension, the Americans in the competitors' stand started to sing. Then, at twenty-three minutes after five o'clock it was announced that Hefferon and Dorando were in sight.

Two minutes later, it was announced that the Italian had entered the grounds and a few minutes later he appeared at the entrance to the Stadium and was greeted by a burst of cheers, but it was immediately perceived that something was wrong. He staggered across the bicycle track, groped blindly forward for a third of the distance to the royal box, and fell. A crowd of officials rushed to him. He was helped up and he started again. In the meantime, twenty yards from the entrance to the grounds, Hayes had overtaken and passed Hefferon. J.M. Andrews, clerk of the course, ran toward the Italian — who had dropped again after another ten yards — and, with a doctor who was accompanying the racer, picked him up.

Dorando reeled across the track like a drunken man, and collapsed again.

Meantime, Hayes had entered the Stadium and was coming on at a fair pace. The officials crowded about Dorando and helped him to his feet and started him again, but a fourth time he staggered and fell. He got upon his feet with difficulty and, with a man on each side of him, was fairly pulled across the line just 21 and 3/5 seconds before Hayes came up.

There never was a pluckier race run, but all in vain.

Dorando, who was almost too weak to answer questions said: "I felt all right until I entered the Stadium. When I heard the people cheering and knew I had nearly won, a thrill passed through me and I felt my strength going. I fell down, but tried to struggle to the tape, but fell again. I never lost consciousness of what was going on, and if the doctor had not ordered the attendants to pick me up, I believe I could have finished unaided."

Dorando is a confectioner, who resides on the island of Capri. He trained himself for the race without any supervision.

Although being picked up and carried had meant automatic disqualification, Dorando received the consolation of a special gold trophy, awarded the next day by Queen Alexandria.

4

The Grey Cup
Hamilton Hijinx

People who follow the history of the Grey Cup, awarded annually to the champions of the Canadian Football League, might be puzzled to see the Hamilton Tigers inscribed as winners of the 1908 title.

CFL history shows the first Grey Cup game took place in 1909.

The answer to the mystery?

The Hamilton Tigers awarded it to themselves.

Hamilton won the Grey Cup in 1915, defeating the Toronto Rowing and Athletic Association 13-7 in the final. The majority of the players on the Tigers were off to Europe and World War I shortly after their victory. Knowing that most of them would never have another shot at winning the Cup again, they held a players caucus and decided to "award themselves" another championship, one for which they felt they deserved recognition earlier.

Since the Tigers had beaten the University of Toronto 21-17 in the 1908 finals, a year before the introduction of the Grey Cup, the Hamiltonians declared they had been "robbed" of their rightful recognition. While the Cup was in their possession in 1915, the players chipped in to have a silversmith inscribe their team as "1908 Grey Cup Champions," thereby baffling CFL historians for decades.

In 1951, the Canadian Rugby Union had the Cup enlarged and the barely-legible inaccuracy was noted. Once the historians traced the story behind the inscription, however, they decided to let it remain rather than destroy a part of the Grey Cup folklore.

5

Rowing
Sculling Stories

Rowing is truly one of the most gruelling sports around. It requires arm, leg and back strength, wind, balance and a ton of endurance.

Canada has done well at this sport in Olympic competition, winning more than twenty medals over the years. One year, though, there was a special medal awarded to a Canadian crew.

It was in 1912. The Canadian crew called the Toronto Argonauts was a great team but trailed badly in the finals of the "eights." Later it was discovered that the Canadians had actually rowed farther than anyone else because the officials had measured the course incorrectly.

Canada made no protest, but the King of Sweden decreed that the Canadian oarsmen should get a special award for good sportsmanship.

Had there been a naturalist award in this sport, it surely would have gone to Australian Henry Pearce in the 1928 Amsterdam Olympics.

Pearce was rowing along furiously in the single sculls, hoping for the gold medal when suddenly he heard the quacking of a flock of ducks as they landed in the path of his boat.

Pearce stopped rowing and pulled in his oars rather than risk hitting the ducks.

After they had paddled out of the way, he bent to the task again. Yes, nice guys can finish first. Not only did Henry Pearce win the race and the gold medal, but he also set a new world record!

6

Jim Thorpe
The greatest athlete ever ?

The greatest ever ? The superlative seems ridiculous at first. How can someone be the greatest ever ? Who knows what's still to come? How does one measure greatness? Are the standards applicable in the modern era?

But if there's a case to be made for a sportsman to be labelled "the greatest ever", the case might be made on Jim Thorpe's behalf.

Jim Thorpe was born in 1888 in a one-room cabin on the banks of the North Canadian River, about ten miles north of Shawnee, Oklahoma in what was then called Indian Territory. He was not a full-blooded Indian; his father was half-Irish, and his mother, a quarter-French. He was supposed to have some Dutch and Welsh blood in his veins. His great-grandfather was Black Hawk, the famous war chief of the Sac and Fox against whom a young captain of volunteers named Abraham Lincoln campaigned in 1832.

Thorpe's mother saw a bright sunlit path leading to the cabin and, following the Indian custom of naming a newborn child after the first sight that met the mother's eye, she called him Wa-Tho-Huch, which means "Bright Path".

His athletic abilities were first revealed at the Carlisle Indian School in Carlisle, Pennsylvania. There he was coached by the famous Glen "Pop" Warner. As an elusive halfback, a fierce tackler on defence and a skilled dropkicker, Thorpe made the college All-America team in 1911 and 1912. Football fans of those days remember him for his team's startling upset of mighty Harvard in 1911, when Thorpe ran 70 yards for a touchdown and kicked four field goals.

A year later, in 1912, the Carlisle Indians upset Army 27-6. In that game, Army had a tough young linebacker named Dwight Eisenhower. Thorpe said later he remembered keeping his eye on Ike: "Good linebacker," he recalled.

Ike too, remembered their gridiron meeting.

"The running of Thorpe was by far the most wonderful and spectacular thing ever seen on our field." Once, Eisenhower and one of his fellow linebackers seemed to have the hard-running Thorpe cornered and they dived for him. He stopped short and the tacklers crashed together. Ike and his teammate both had to leave the game.

The cadets in the stands, although sadly humbled, gave Thorpe a rousing ovation for his spectacular play that day.

Later that season, on Thanksgiving Day against Brown, Thorpe played his last game in school. It was in a snowstorm, but again Thorpe put on a great show. He scored three touchdowns, kicked two field goals, and set up the other scores as Carlisle won 32-0. After that performance, Referee Mike Thompson called Thorpe "the greatest football player — ever."

It is debatable whether Thorpe was better at football or track and field. His amazing exploits at the 1912 Olympic Games in Stockholm are the stuff that legend is made of. Competing against the best all-round athletes in the world, Thorpe won both the pentathalon and the decathalon, something no other athlete has ever done. It was quite fitting that King Gustavus of Sweden, in awarding Thorpe the gold medals, uttered the historic remark, "You, sir, are the greatest athlete in the world."

The next year, however, it was revealed that Thorpe had played professional baseball briefly in 1909 with a couple of teams in North Carolina. He had played under his own name and had collected $15.00 a week. Still, it made him a professional. The Amateur Athletic Union revoked his status and the International Olympic Committee took back his medals. There was a storm of protest on Thorpe's behalf and appeals that lasted until his death in 1953, and for thirty years after.

"I was just a dumb Indian kid," Thorpe told a writer in 1952, "How was I to know that playing baseball for money made me a professional in football and track?"

After the Olympic debacle, Thorpe signed to play pro baseball in the major leagues. He played for the New York Giants for a few years, but ran afoul of a hard-nosed manager there and was sent to Boston in 1919. Despite his reputation for not being able to hit a curve ball, he batted .327. But his "hell-raising" lifestyle and nonchalant attitude toward practices got him sent to the minor leagues where he languished for four years before quitting the game. During most of those years, Thorpe also played football, helping build a team called the Canton Bulldogs to respectability. In 1920, he helped found what became the National Football League and was its first president. He also played for several teams in that young league from 1921 to 1926.

When Thorpe's playing days ended, however, he had nothing productive to which to turn. For a time he was able to capitalize on his reputation by lecturing, taking bit parts in films, and so on. But at one point he was reduced to digging ditches at $4 a day. Funds were raised to assist him, but he never became a wealthy man.

In 1950 the Associated Press polled nearly four hundred sportswriters and broadcasters to determine the best athletes for the first half of the twentieth century. In football, Thorpe was the winner over Red Grange by 170 votes to 138. Another poll was taken to determine the greatest male athlete of all, amateur or professional. Here again, Thorpe's name led all the rest, with Babe Ruth, Jack Dempsey, Ty Cobb and Bobby Jones falling far behind in the balloting. Even while he lived, Warner Brothers made a feature movie about his life.

When he died in 1953, his passing rated Column One, Page One of the "New York Times." President Eisenhower and other dignitaries wrote messages of condolences.

Jim Thorpe, the greatest athlete ever, was buried among his people, the Thunderbird Clan of the Sac and Fox Nation, at Shawnee, Oklahoma, near where he was born.

In 1973, his amateur status was restored, and in 1982, Thorpe's Olympic medals were returned to his family.

7

George Gipp
An Idol's Remark

The records show that as a freshman football player for Notre Dame in 1916, George Gipp once drop-kicked the ball 62 yards for the winning field goal against Western Michigan. The records do not say how many billiard balls he dropped into the side-pockets at Hullie and Mike's pool-room in downtown South Bend. For Gipp, football was a delightful game, college a delightful diversion but pool a delightful livelihood. He wasn't quite the clean-living hero Ronald Reagan made him out to be in the film, *Knute Rockne-All American.*

In 1917 Gipp led Notre Dame to victory over Army. The following season he was a standout on the first Rockne-coached Notre Dame team. In 1920 he was expelled, but ultimately passed a make-up exam and got back into Notre Dame.

He gambled heavily on his own team, and continued a fast-living, pool-shooting lifestyle, passing up on sleep as if it were something for other people to worry about but not him. And through all this he was one of the most gifted football players of his time.

But the late-night pace took its toll. George Gipp was obviously sick through most of the 1920 season. Naturally, it was his greatest season.

On October 20th, 1920, George Gipp coughed his way past Army, gaining 124 yards rushing, passing for 96 yards and running back punts and kickoffs for another 112. He was plainly the difference as Notre Dame whipped Army, 27-17. When he left the field that afternoon, the entire Corps of Army Cadets gave him a grudging ovation.

Gipp's health continued to deteriorate after the Army game. He helped beat Purdue and Indiana in flamboyant fashion while managing to work in a three-day "bender" in Chicago. Against Northwestern, he was obviously ill and played little. When his team played the final game of the season that year against the Michigan Aggies, George Gipp lay dying of pneumonia in St. Joseph's Hospital. The end came on December 14th, 1920.

Eight years later, George Gipp played a key role in the game that, perhaps more than any other, gained millions of uncommitted football fans and focused their attention on annual Notre Dame-Army matchups.

Rockne's 1928 team had won just five of nine games, the worst record in Rockne's career. Army, led by All-American Chris Cagel, was a huge favorite. But after this game no Army-Notre Dame match-up would ever be the same.

Notre Dame won it 12-6, with the winning touchdown pass being caught by a reserve player who later came to be known as John "One-Play" O'Brien. Despite the drama of that long afternoon at Yankee Stadium, the real story took place in the Notre Dame locker room. It didn't become known to the public until 48 hours later; on Monday morning readers in New York opened their sports pages to see this report by Francis Wallace in the Daily News:

"Football people knew Rockne would fire up his boys in his speech before the game. This is what he told them:
'On his deathbed, George Gipp told me that some day when the time came, he wanted me to ask a Notre Dame team to beat Army for him.'"

The Notre Dame players, for whom Gipp was legend, were so inspired, they went out and beat Army. The Notre Dame star, Jack Chevigny, is said to have thrown the ball in the air after he scored the tying touchdown, looked toward the heavens and shouted: "That's one for the Gipper!"

That is the way it happened. With time, however, the story moved further and further from actual fact and into the realm of myth. Suddenly, George Gipp became the very essence of spirit, loyalty and the American Dream. The qualities people began to ascribe to him far transcended his magnificent abilities as a football player. The pre-game speech by Rockne and the thought of Gipp asking for a Notre Dame win over Army with his dying breath took on supernatural aspects for the Notre Dame fans.

With Ronald Reagan telling it to Pat O'Brien and O'Brien telling it to the whole cast in the Hollywood version every time they replay the movie on the Late Late Show, how could the battle cry, "Win one for the Gipper," not become a standard?

8

Rowing
Life After Olympic Gold

The winners of the gold medal in rowing at the Paris Olympics in 1924 were the scullers from Yale University. The Yale crew sailed for France full of anticipation as the Paris Games would be the biggest ever held up to that time, with more than three thousand athletes from 44 nations entered. Among the other American favorites entered that year was the great swimmer, Johnny Weismuller, who went on to win two gold medals.

The Yale oarsmen were favored, but were far from overconfident. Their coach, Ed Leader, wanted nothing less than perfection.

The coach insisted on morning and afternoon naps and a 9:30 curfew at night.

Proper nutrition was also a major issue with Coach Leader. When the Yale crew first arrived in Paris, they were shocked by the "continental breakfast" offered them each morning.

"Our breakfast the first morning," recalled one rower, "was a shrivelled orange — as big around as a half-dollar — a croissant, and a curl of butter."

Neither was Leader happy with the lodgings offered by the Games' organizers. He moved his team out of the concrete barracks and into a large apartment in the attractive Paris suburb known as "Saint-Germaine-en-Laye." Beside the building was a famous restaurant called "Francois Premier." There, with the bill being footed by Yale alumni and other supporters, his crew ate and rested very well.

The Yale men breezed to their gold medal victory on the evening of July 17th, the eight men rowing in perfect sync along the two-thousand metre course on the Seine River. Their winning margin was an incredible one-hundred metres over the nearest boat.

While rowing is very much a team sport, Ben Spock was recognized that year as the leader of the Yale crew. The Boston Post reported that Spock was "the best individual performer. In all the races in 1924, Spock passed the stroke down his side of the shell with such smoothness and accuracy that he kept all forward of him in line."

Each of the members of the victorious crew was presented with a gold medal and, of course, each man assured himself of a lasting place in the annals of Yale athletics. "I really did succeed in sports beyond my wildest dreams," says Spock.

Spock finished his degree the following year and stayed for two years of graduate studies at Yale Medical School. Later, he went to New York and finished his medical studies at Columbia University. After practicing at the famed Mayo Clinic and holding university posts in Pittsburgh and Cleveland, Benjamin Spock was carving out a distinguished career by the summer of 1943. That year, a man named Donald Geddes, a budding editor of paperback books, asked Dr. Spock if he'd like to write a book about child care. Spock accepted, but due to the demands on his schedule, he wasn't able to finish the book until late in 1945.

Called *The Common Sense Book of Baby Care*, it began to appear in drug stores, supermarkets and bookstores across America and sold at a remarkable rate. Soon, the sales were being measured in the millions and the book had an amazing impact on child rearing. Studies show that one out of every four children born in the United States since 1945 has been raised by parents who used the book as a major source of guidance.

9

Ronald Reagan
Crying Foul

The former U.S. President, Ronald Reagan, achieved some fame as an actor in his days before politics, but first started out as a radio announcer at station W-H-O in Des Moines, Iowa.

He did all kinds of announcing, but was best known for his sports-casting, which he preferred to his other assignments. He became especially associated with baseball, a game he had never been able to play, or even to watch in a big-league city.

In fact, Reagan was not even seeing the games he described in vivid detail to a growing audience through the baseball seasons of the Depression. He was three hundred miles away from the Chicago games he was calling "live", while working at the radio station, looking over a telegraph relay from the ballpark.

"Looking through the window I would see the telegraph man, Curly, with his headphones on, start typing. This was my cue to start talking.

It would go something like this: 'the pitcher (whatever his name happened to be) has the sign, he's coming out of the windup, here's the pitch,' and at that moment, Curly would slip me the blank. It might contain the information S2C, and without pause I would translate this into 'It's a called strike breaking over the inside corner, making it two strikes on the batter.' If the Cubs were in the field, I would continue while I waited for the next dot and dash, saying, 'Harntett returns the ball to Lon Warneke, Warneke is dusting his hands on the resin, steps back up to the mound, is getting the sign again from Hartnett, here's the wind up and the pitch...'"

Over six hundred times Reagan went through this elaborate process. The daily demands of this "think-out-loud" technique called for quick wits as well as a lively imagination. That is the point of Reagan's most famous radio story:

"I saw Curly start to type so I finished the windup and had Dizzy Dean sending a ball on its way to the plate. I took the slip from Curly, and found myself faced with the terse note: 'The wire has gone dead.' I had a ball on the way to the plate and there was no way to call it back. At the same time, I was convinced that a ball game tied up in the ninth inning was no time to tell my audience we had lost contact with the game and we would have to play recorded music. I knew of only one thing that wouldn't show up in the score column and betray me — a foul ball! So I had Augie foul this pitch down the left field line. I looked expectantly at Curly. He just shrugged helplessly, so I had Augie foul off another one and still another; then he fouled one back into the box seats. I described in detail how a red-headed kid scrambled after it and got himself a souvenir. Then he fouled one into the upper deck that just missed being a home run. He fouled off pitches for six minutes and forty-five seconds until I lost count. I began to be frightened that maybe I was establishing a new world record for a fellow staying at bat and hitting fouls, and this could betray me. Yet I was so far into it that I didn't dare reveal that the wire had gone dead. My voice was rising in pitch and threatening to crack — and then, bless him, Curly started typing. I clutched at the slip of paper. It said: 'Galan popped out on the first ball pitched.' Not in my game he didn't — he popped out after practically making a career of foul balls."

Obviously, Ronald Reagan became adept early in life at leading people to believe he knew what was going on. It was a skill he was to call upon again later in life, in another career.

10

Eddie Shore
Old Scarface

Name the player who absorbed the most stiches in his professional hockey career.

Although one of the few areas not covered by the National Hockey League's vast data bank is "stitches absorbed," hockey historians generally agree that *Eddie Shore* was cut, sliced, punctured and generally wounded more than any other big-leaguer. Shore battled his way through a turbulent 15-year career that would have driven insurance underwriters to distraction. Dubbed "The Edmonton Express," Shore emerged as one of the NHL's original stars. He launched his NHL stint with the Boston Bruins in 1926, playing a death-defying style of hockey that did absolutely no good for his fuselage.

In a single contest against the hated Montreal Maroons, Shore suffered a lacerated cheekbone, a two-inch cut over his left eye, a broken nose, three broken teeth and two black eyes. In addition he was knocked cold for 14 minutes during the game. Shore did not miss the following contest.

Another time he broke three ribs after crashing into a goal post. Instead of leaving the Bruins to go to the hospital, Shore slipped away from the doctor, caught a train to Montreal where the next game would be played and scored two goals the following night!

It has been estimated that Shore was embroidered with more than 800 stitches, many of which were required as a result of fights inspired by Eddie, himself. He set an NHL record for penalty minutes in just his second season as a big-leaguer. But despite Shore's reputation around the NHL as a villain (except, of course, in Boston), he was not your big, clumsy goon. Four times Shore won the Hart Trophy as the league's most valuable player and he was a First Team All-Star no less than seven times.

11

Buddy Hassett
An Irish Lullabye

First baseman Buddy Hassett played for the Brooklyn Dodgers in the late 1930's when Casey Stengel was managing the club. Hassett's voice was so highly regarded that he could sing professionally, but he was also a good ball player.

Once, when the Dodgers were riding the rails to their spring training base in Florida, they encountered a mother and her infant in the club car. The baby, apparently suffering from colic, cried incessantly from Newark to Baltimore.

Stengel finally got an idea; he suggested that Hassett and his dulcet tones might lull the baby to sleep.

"Madam," said Stengel, "I'm the manager of the Brooklyn Dodgers and this is my left-handed tenor singer, Buddy Hassett. He'll now sing your infant to sleep."

Without hesitation Hassett crooned a chorus of "Mighty Lak a Rose" and before he could reach the finale the baby was peacefully dozing in his mother's arms.

Stengel then returned to his seat and turned to one of the sportswriters who had lately been critical of his managing and observed: "I have my critics, but they can't say I don't get the most out of my players."

12

Al Moore
Arms and the Man

New York Giants manager John McGraw once chewed out an outfielder for making a perfect throw to the plate.

Al Moore, an outfielder with a strong arm, was once sent in by McGraw in the late innings. With a runner on second, the batter singled to left. Moore, throwing all the way to the plate without a bounce, nailed the runner at home and ended the inning.

The Giants fans cheered lustily, but McGraw was unimpressed. Instead, he said to Moore, "I thought I explained to you that I always want throws from the outfield to take one hop, in case a cutoff was necessary. You probably think you've made a fine throw. You've heard those fans cheering and you think you're big stuff. I'll show you how big you are in relation to the team.

"Suppose I put a sign up which says, 'tomorrow afternoon there will be a throwing exhibition by Al Moore at Polo Grounds.' How many fans do you think it would attract? You wouldn't get fifty. I could and should fine you fifty, but I won't. In the future, just remember that the fans came here to see the Giants play, not to see Al Moore exercise his arm."

Al Moore repeated this story later on for the benefit of a young rookie named Joe DiMaggio.

13

Yogi Berra
The Nickname

There are a couple of former baseball players who have come to be household names even to people who began following the game long after

these guys played.
I'm speaking of Yogi Berra and Joe Garagiola.
They were childhood buddies, having grown up across the street from one another in St. Louis in the late 1930's and early 40's. Both went on to play in the major leagues, both as catchers, and while Garagiola went on to fame as a broadcaster, Berra went on to manage both the Yankees and the Mets to pennant-winning seasons, and still coaches now with Houston.

Garagiola remembers how the famous nickname "Yogi" came about:

His real name is Lawrence, and all us kids called him "Lawdie."

He was the best at every sport. He could throw and kick a football better than anyone. He was best at baseball, at street hockey; no matter what the sport, there was never any question who the first pick would be when we were choosing up sides. Whoever won the hand-over-hand duel up the neck of the bat for first pick always chirped out, "I'll take Lawdie!"

He could have been a football player, given his skill at that sport as a youth. We had a great scam for getting hold of good footballs to play with. In those days, the St. Louis University team used to play at a stadium about a mile from where we lived. When practice was on, we'd line up about 30 yards apart on the street outside the stadium fence. Whenever a ball came over, we'd get it to "Lawdie" right away 'cause he could throw the farthest. He'd throw a long pass to me, I'd throw to the next kid down the line and so on. The equipment managers from the St. Louis University football team never had a chance.

"Lawdie" was also the designated punter when we played football in the street. He'd do the kicking for both teams when it was fourth down. That was because he could kick straight and we didn't have the budget back then for broken windows.

But, the "Yogi" came as a result of his distinctive walk. (If you've ever seen him walk out to the mound to talk to a pitcher you know what "distinctive" means, and after seeing that walk once, you never had to check the number on his back to identify him. It was said he was the only guy known who'd scuff his does on the inside.)

Bobby Hoffman, who later played for the New York Giants, was at a movie once and saw a scene where an East Indian yogi charmed a snake out of a basket. When the yogi stood up and walked away from the camera, Hoffman said, "That yogi walks just like Lawdie."

The nickname caught and stuck, so much so that his Mom, an Italian lady who spoke almost no English, also eventually called him "Yogi."

14

Foster Hewitt
A Voice from Home

When the Second World War began, and Canada became involved, a wave of patriotism not unmixed with panic took over public affairs.

Strangely enough, one of the first targets was hockey. The attack came not from Ottawa, busy making decisions in all directions, but from Manitoba. Mr. Justice J.E. Adamson, chairman of the Manitoba division of the National War Services Board, refused passports to six Canadian players about to leave to play for the Detroit Red Wings. His reasoning was that able-bodied Canadians should not be leaving Canada in wartime to work in the United States.

This move prompted a furious debate. Newspapers, politicians and the general public began taking sides. Should hockey go on as normal during wartime? The Globe and Mail editorialized that young Canadians should be shooting rifles rather than pucks. An Ontario judge declaimed, "When I read the sports page I see great Goliaths of men in the wrong uniforms. All civilization is at stake and we go on as if we were at peace."

But, about that time some far-sighted people in the military began to be heard. While no one could foresee the needs of the future, they said, the single most popular sport in the country should not be taking so much heat. The Maple Leafs and Foster Hewitt and the other teams in the NHL, along with Imperial Oil as the sponsor of the Saturday night radio broadcasts from Toronto, had combined to produce the greatest single national once-a-week get-together Canada had ever known. So hockey should go on. And so should the hockey broadcasts. Hockey players would not be immune to call-ups for military service, but it was reasoned that home-front morale could only be worsened if hockey, one of the national preoccupations and ways of escaping the worries of war for a few hours, was removed.

Wartime hockey broadcasts doubled Foster Hewitt's workload.

Dozens of war-connected appeals and government announcements went out on the hockey broadcasts. One of the most dramatic came in December of 1941 when the Japanese attacked Pearl Harbor and the west coast of North America immediately became a potential front line. Canada was badly prepared. Troops were rushed to Vancouver Island and the RCAF stepped up its coastal patrols. But, the whole coast-watching effort was hampered by a shortage of high-powered binoculars. A call went out across the country on Foster Hewitt's hockey broadcast. From that one mention on a Saturday night Leaf's game, more than 1,100 pairs of binoculars poured in to the RCAF. Of those, some 400 were powerful enough to be of use. Foster Hewitt told his audience the following Saturday night, "That's enough binoculars."

About then, the idea came up that Foster's hockey broadcasts could be recorded and packaged for re-broadcast to the servicemen overseas, via the British Broadcasting Corporation. Foster would broadcast the games, then head back to the radio station, put together a condensed, half-hour version of the highlights; the goals, the fights, the big body-checks, and he made efforts to mention the hometowns of the players. At first, some of these game tapes were actually flown to England on RCAF planes. Later, they were shortwaved over, and hours later, Foster's play-by-play was piped around the world on the BBC's Empire service.

This was a timely operation as it allowed Foster to send to the Canadian personnel overseas the excitement of the Stanley Cup Final in 1942 where the Leafs roared back from three games down to beat Detroit. It was considered one of the great comebacks in sports history and Foster had described it all in thrilling detail. And 1942 was a particularly dark time in the war; the Japanese were overrunning the Pacific, German and Italian forces were holding most of mainland Europe and North Africa, German artillery and tanks were everywhere in Russia and the Ukraine. There didn't seem to be a ray of light anywhere.

Hewitt got letters from places like China, India, Australia, New Guinea, Guadalcanal and Tobruk, thanking him for a "touch of home." The officer commanding the Royal Regiment of Canada, Lieutenant-Colonel Arthur H. Fraser, DSO, summed up Hewitt's impact when he told a civilian audience, "More than anything, the men in England want the hockey broadcasts, then cigarettes, then your parcels."

15

Barbara Ann Scott
Bombin' around Bytown

Barbara Ann Scott was Canada's first modern-day figure skating champion. A striking young woman from Ottawa, she began skating at age six, and at ten became the youngest skater ever to pass the gold figures test. She blossomed into a two-time world champion in 1947 and 1948 and an Olympic gold medal winner in 1948. She was nearly disqualified from the Olympics, however, because of a gift given her by her hometown of Ottawa. Before the 1948 Winter Games, the city honoured her with a yellow convertible car. The Olympic Committee said that verged on being paid to compete, and Scott had to give the car back. She later said it was the saddest thing she ever had to do.

Although denied money and gifts while amateurs, some champion skaters have been able to carve out lucrative careers. In her first ever Winter Olympics in 1924, an 11-year-old Norwegian girl with a big

30

smile and a friendly wave placed 8th in women's figure skating. Four years later, she won the gold medal and went on to win the gold on two more occasions. Eventually, she moved to Hollywood and enjoyed quite a career in the movies. In fact, Sonja Heine still holds the world record for the most post-Olympic earnings by an athlete as a result of her sports popularity — more than $47 million from films and ice shows.

16

Al Melgard
No Requests Please

An organist at a National Hockey League rink once was censured by the League President. Who was the organist? Why was he censured? And who was the President who criticized him?

Al Melgard had been organist for the Chicago Black Hawks since 1927 through the 1970's. Unlike organists at other NHL rinks, Melgard had a zany streak and frequently would play tunes appropriate to the doing on the ice. For example, if a couple of players started a fight and then went into a clinch, Melgard would play "Let Me Call You Sweetheart" and "Put Your Arms Around Me Honey." When a player got a penalty, Melgard would bang out "The Prisoner's Song." If there was high sticking in progress he'd play "Lay That Pistol Down, Babe" or "The Sabre Dance."

"One night," said Bill Tobin, one time manager of the Black Hawks, "someone fired a dead squirrel from the balcony to the ice surface. It landed close to Pat Egan, the Boston Bruins defenseman. As soon as Pat saw it, he raised his stick like a gun and went 'bang-bang.' Melgard immediately started to play 'A-Hunting We Will Go.' When the cleaners came out and removed the deceased squirrel from the ice, Melgard added solemnity to the occasion by playing the 'Death March'."

For decades Melgard played his ditties with impunity. But in the 1940's some officials began getting a big edgy. Referee King Clancy objected to the organist playing "Three Blind Mice" when he and the two linesmen skated on the ice. "It's tough enough refereeing here without the organist getting the crowd worked up before the game starts," said Clancy.

Manager Tobin asked Melgard to refrain from playing "Three Blind Mice," which he did. Next time Clancy appeared in Chicago he was greeted with a rendition of "For He's a Jolly Good Fellow."

But the irrepressible Melgard returned to the "Three Blind Mice" routine in the 1960's and, this time, NHL President Clarence Campbell intervened and suggested that discretion would be more appropriate. Melgard agreed and, from then on, the organ music emanating from his Wurlitzer was pleasant enough to suit even the tastes of the league's chief executive.

17

King Clancy
Clancy Classics

One of hockey's best loved men was Francis Michael (King) Clancy. With his passing in 1987 came a gushing of funny, touching anecdotes as hockey people from several eras paid tribute and remembered him fondly. But, before his death, there were many great King Clancy yarns spun from his own recollections. Here are two of his best:

A player with the Maple Leafs in the 1930's, Clancy was a small and feisty defenceman. He often mixed it up with tough customers from the other teams, but rarely successfully. An oft-repeated scene in a Leafs game was Clancy getting into a scrap, soon ending up on the bottom and taking a beating until teammate Charlie Conacher came to his aid and broke things up.

It was facetiously said that in his career, Clancy had been in a thousand hockey fights but had never won one. He begged to differ in a TV interview in the early 1980's.

"Oh, I won one all right; it was against Eddie Shore," said King to CBC interviewer Harry Brown.

"Really ... now, Eddie Shore?" said Brown, looking rather skeptical at the thought of the wiry Clancy beating the feared Bruins strongman.

"Yeah sure..." said Clancy with a twinkle in his eye.

"He was on his knees one time as I was going by and I belted him."

Another classic King Clancy story comes from his second life in hockey, as a referee in the 1940's.

"I was handling a Rangers-Blackhawks game in Madison Square Garden one night and one of the Chicago players broke through the defence and was tripped so I blew my whistle for a penalty. But just as I blew the whistle he took a shot as he was falling ... and the puck went in. Well I knew I was in for a rhubarb, but I never even hesitated a second, even as the Ranger players were going crazy."

"Hey Clancy, you blew the whistle," they yelled.

"Sure did," he called over his shoulder, his mind racing. He skated over, took the puck out of the net and headed to centre ice.

"Always do when there's a goal scored," he lied to the Ranger players.

Needless to say, each time there was a goal scored for the rest of the game and any time Clancy handled a game in Madison Square Garden, he kept up his newly-initiated routine, dutifully blowing his whistle and going over to take the puck out of the net himself.

18

Monarchy and the Maple Leafs
First Impressions

When did British royalty make its first appearance at a National Hockey League game?

On the night of October 13, 1951 Their Royal Highnesses, Princess Elizabeth and The Duke of Edinburgh visited Maple Leaf Gardens for a match between the Maple Leafs and Chicago Black Hawks.

Prior to the arrival of the royal visitors Ted (Teeder) Kennedy, the Toronto captain, pondered the protocol of a formal introduction to the royal pair. He wondered whether he would remember to bow, what to call them and what to say.

Fortunately, Princess Elizabeth and Prince Philip quickly put everyone at ease. The formal introductions were friendly and informal. When Leafs manager Conn Smythe introduced Kennedy, Princess Elizabeth, with the Maple Leaf Gardens program tucked under her left arm, smiled graciously and extended her hand.

"How do you do," she said.

"Your Royal Highness," Kennedy replied as he took her hand and bowed his head.

Ed Fitkin was publicist for the Maple Leafs at the time of the visit. He vividly recalled the reaction of Princess Elizabeth once the contest began.

Fitkin: "Once the hockey game got underway the Princess came alive with animation. Her eyes sparkled as she intently followed the play. She recoiled slightly at the heavy bodychecks and she talked and smiled with Conn Smythe frequently. She was enjoying herself. So was the Duke. And their reactions were typical of hockey fans everywhere.

"It was evident, as the minutes ticked by and the Royal couple continued to sit spellbound by the action on the ice that the 15-minute period allotted for the visit to Maple Leaf Gardens was going to be exceeded. They completely captivated everyone who came, saw and were conquered by Royalty's first visit to Maple Leaf Gardens."

19

The Olympic Marathon
A Tradition of Greatness

Olympic marathoners have always been a special breed, in ancient and in modern times. Consider first the origins of the event.

In 490 B.C., Pheidippides, a soldier and champion runner, fought the Persians who were trying to conquer the Greek town of Marathon. When the battle was won, Pheidippides ran the 42 kilometres (26 miles) from Marathon to Athens to give the great news. When he arrived, he shouted: "Rejoice, we conquer." Then he dropped dead.

His feat was honoured during the first modern Olympics in 1896 with a 42-kilometre race for men, which was called, "the marathon." It was held in Greece and after all the events but one had been held, not a single Greek athlete had won a medal.

The final event of the Olympics was the marathon, a gruelling run over dusty, rocky roads under the blazing hot sun. One of the 25 runners was a scrawny Greek shepherd named Spiridon Louis, who wanted to show the world that the old glory of Greece was alive.

The race began. One by one the experienced runners collapsed from the heat. Spiridon kept going though, until finally there was only one runner, a Frenchman, ahead of him. With a short distance to go in the marathon, the Greeks screaming his name, Spiridon Louis sprinted past the Frenchman to win the gold medal for the host country in the first modern Olympics.

The marathon was supposed to remain at the 42-kilometre (26-mile) distance, true to the length of Pheidippides' heroic run, but, in the 1908

Olympics in London, organizers added 352 metres (385 yards). The extra distance was tacked on so that the finish would take place in front of the royal viewing box.

Down through the Olympics, there have been numerous heroic marathoners. In 1952, in Helsinki, Czechoslovak runner Emil Zatopek did something no long-distance runner had ever done. He won the gold medal in the 5,000-metre race, the 10,000-metre race and in the marathon, a race he had never run before. During the marathon, he kept turning to his closest competitor and asking, "Are we going fast enough?"

In Rome, in 1960, Abede Bikila of Ethiopia stunned spectators by running the entire marathon, and winning it, in bare feet. He earned another gold medal in the marathon four years later in Tokyo, even though he was still recovering from an appendix operation.

Sadly, he was later crippled in a car accident and can no longer walk.

For a long time there was no marathon for women. It was believed to be too gruelling a run; there were fears that if women were allowed to run the marathon, the toll on them would be so great they might not be able to bear children.

Eventually, these fears were proved to be nonsense and women began running marathon races. Still, it wasn't until 1984 that the Olympics included a women's marathon.

Both races are always run on the final day of the Olympics and they remain one of the most riveting spectacles in the Games.

20

Camille Henry
Bench-warmer of the Year

This player was a bench-warmer for most of his first National Hockey League season, yet, incredibly, he was named winner of the Calder Trophy as the Rookie of the Year. What was his name?

Camille Henry was one of the skinniest players ever to don a major league uniform. He was nicknamed "The Eel" and sometimes appeared so fragile one wondered how he even survived a single game, let alone an entire season.

Henry learned his hockey in Quebec City and starred for the Junior Quebec Citadelles in the early 1950's when he was invited to the New York Rangers training camp in the Fall of 1953. Henry did not expect to make the NHL club because he had had no previous big-league experience and none in the pros either. But on the afternoon of the first preseason game he received a telephone call from general manager Frank Boucher.

"Max Bentley, the Rangers veteran center, had gotten sick a few hours before game time," Henry remembered, "and Boucher called me up and told me I was going to play instead. By the end of the pre-season schedule I had more points than any other center on the team.

"When we were breaking camp, Boucher called me into his office — I thought he was going to tell me he was sending me down to the minor league team — and he said to me 'Cammy, I think you can make the NHL. I have my 20 players right now but I'd like to carry you with the team because I think you can learn a lot just from watching.'

"The season started in Detroit and I didn't dress. In the second period Dean Prentice dislocated his shoulder, giving me my chance. The next night we were in Chicago and Boucher told me to dress. We won 5-2; I scored a goal and got an assist."

But Boucher made good on his promise to use Henry only sparingly. The Rangers boss kept his skinny center on the bench for long periods, employing him only on the power play with Max Bentley.

"I remember one night we were in Detroit," Henry recalled, "and Max told me he was going to score a goal against the Red Wings. This was when they had their greatest team with Gordie Howe, Ted Lindsay, Alex Delvecchio, Red Kelly and Terry Sawchuk. So I told him if he was going to score one, I was going to score one, too.

"In the second period we had a power play and Max was on the ice. He took the puck on his stick and skated all the way down the ice through Howe, Lindsay, Kelly, Bob Goldham and then put a move on Terry

Sawchuk and scored a goal. He skated over to the bench and winked. I said 'Don't forget about me' and he said 'Don't worry, you'll score.'

"We were out on the ice about a minute later when Max got the puck again. He started a mad dash toward the Detroit goal, right through their defense, just like the first time. He got right in front of Sawchuk, pulled him out and had him cold turkey, but instead of shooting he passed the puck over to where I had come down the left side. There was no way in the world I could have missed, so I put the puck in the net just that easy."

Despite his part-time duty Henry finished the year with 24 goals and 39 points and the Calder Trophy as the league's top rookie. It was the start of a 17-year career in which Henry also won The Lady Byng Trophy (1958) as a Ranger and later starred for the Chicago Black Hawks and St. Louis Blues.

What few people remember about Henry is that in the year that he won the Calder Trophy as a part-time player he beat out the immortal Jean Beliveau of the Montreal Canadiens for the rookie prize although Beliveau was a full-time skater all season.

21

Sir Edmund Hillary
Everest

The story of man's first ascent of the world's highest mountain in 1954 is best told by Hillary himself:

We seemed to have been going for a very long time and my confidence was fast evaporating. Bump followed bump with maddening regularity. A patch of shingle barred our way, and I climbed dully up it and started cutting steps around another bump. And then I realized that this was the last bump, for ahead of me the ridge dropped steeply away in a great corniced curve, and out in the distance I could see the pastel shades and fleecy clouds of the highlands of Tibet.

To my right a slender snow ridge climbed up to a snowy dome about forty feet above our heads. But all the way along the ridge the thought had haunted me that the summit might be the crest of a cornice. It was too late to take risks now. I asked Tenzing to belay me strongly, and I started cutting a cautious line of steps up the ridge. Peering from side to side and thrusting with my ice-axe, I tried to discover a possible cornice, but everything seemed solid and firm. I waved Tenzing up to me. A few more whacks of the ice-axe, a few very weary steps, and we were on the summit of Everest.

It was 11:30 a.m. My first sensation was one of relief — relief that the long grind was over; that the summit had been reached before our oxygen supplies had dropped to a critical level; and relief that in the end the mountain had been kind to us in having a pleasantly rounded cone for its summit instead of a fearsome and unapproachable cornice. But mixed with the relief was a vague sense of astonishment that I should have been the lucky one to attain the ambition of so many brave and determined climbers. It seemed difficult at first to grasp that we'd got there. I was too tired and too conscious of the long way down to safety really to feel any great elation. But as the fact of our success thrust itself more clearly into my mind, I felt a quiet glow of satisfaction spread through my body — a satisfaction less vociferous but more powerful than I had ever felt on a mountain top before. I turned and looked at Tenzing. Even beneath his oxygen mask and the icicles hanging from his hair, I could see his infectious grin of sheer delight. I held out my hand, and in silence we shook in good Anglo-Saxon fashion. But this was not enough for Tenzing, and impulsively he threw his arm around my shoulders and we thumped each other on the back in mutual congratulations.

But we had no time to waste! First I must take some photographs and then we'd hurry down. I turned off my oxygen and took the set off my back. I remembered all the warnings I'd had of the possible fatal consequences of this, but for some reason felt quite confident that nothing serious would result. I took my camera out of the pocket of my wind-proof and clumsily opened it with my thickly gloved hands. I clipped on the lenshood and ultra-violet filter and then shuffled down the ridge a little so that I could get the summit into my viewfinder. Tenzing had been waiting patiently, but now, at my request, he unfurled the flags wrapped around his ice-axe and standing on the summit held them above his head. Clad in all his bulky equipment and with the flags flapping furiously in the wind, he made a dramatic picture, and the thought drifted through my mind that this photograph should be a good one if it came out at all. I didn't worry about getting Tenzing to take a photograph of me — as far as I knew, he had never taken a photograph before and the summit of Everest was hardly the place to show him how.

I climbed up to the top again and started taking a photographic record in every direction.

One scene was of particular interest. Almost under our feet, it seemed, was the famous North Col and the East Rongbuk glacier, where so many epic feats of courage and endurance were performed by the earlier British Everest Expeditions. Part of the ridge up which they had established their high camps was visible, but the last thousand feet, which had proved such a formidable barrier, was concealed from our view as its rock slopes dropped away with frightening abruptness from the summit snow pyramid. It was a sobering thought to remember how often these men had reached 28,000 feet without the benefits of our modern equipment and reasonably efficient oxygen sets. Inevitably my thoughts turned to Mallory and Irvine, who had lost their lives on the mountain thirty years before. With little hope I looked around for some sign that they had reached the summit, but could see nothing.

Meanwhile Tenzing had also been busy. On the summit he'd scratched out a little hole in the snow, and in this he placed some small offerings of food — some biscuits, a piece of chocolate, and a few sweets — a small gift to the Gods of Chomolungma which all devout Buddhists (as Tenzing is) believe to inhabit the summit of this mountain. Besides the food, I placed the little cross that John Hunt had given me on the South Col. Strange companions, no doubt, but symbolical at least of the spiritual strength and peace that all peoples have gained from the mountains.

Bannister and Landy
The Miracle Mile

Long before the opening parade of athletes at the 1954 British Empire Games in Vancouver, the meeting of milers Roger Bannister of England and John Landy of Australia had been labelled as the premier event of the quadrennial sports festival.

The middle-distance event at Empire Stadium more than lived up to its billing.

It was August 7th. Landy held the world record at three minutes, 57.9 seconds; Bannister had been the first man to break the four minute barrier three months earlier.

Bannister did his final training race on the lush grounds of a golf course at the University of British Columbia. He had a cold in his chest and worried about his attitude as race time grew near.

"I am certain that one's feelings at the last minute before a race matter most." Bannister later wrote. "Confidence that has been supreme until the final moment can be lost quite suddenly."

There were eight finalists in the mile, including Rich Ferguson of Leaside, Ontario. But this day belonged to Bannister and Landy.

Bill Baillie of New Zealand took the early lead in the race and Bannister stayed back in third place, behind Landy. The Australian took over the lead and completed the first lap seven yards ahead of Bannister. Landy stayed ahead at the half and three-quarter marks and Bannister recalls thinking the Australian was going to break the world record again.

Quickening his stride, Bannister was at Landy's shoulder like a shadow, his strides becoming more painful with the quick tempo.

"It was incredible that in a race at this speed he should start a finishing burst 300 yards from the tape," Bannister said. "If Landy did not slacken soon, I would be finished." Bannister tried to convince himself that Landy was tiring, and decided that if he was to pass Landy, it would have to be on the final bend.

In a moment now commemorated by a bronze statue in front of Empire Stadium, Bannister and Landy made racing history.

"Just before the end of the last bend, I flung myself past Landy," Bannister recalled. "As I did so, I saw him glance inwards over his opposite shoulder. This tiny act of his held great significance. The moment he looked around he was unprotected against me and so lost a valuable fraction of a second in his response to my challenge. It was my tremendous luck that these two happenings — his turning around and my final spurt — came absolutely simultaneously."

Bannister took the lead with 70 yards to go and managed to hold it to the tape in what was called the "Miracle Mile."

Bannister won the gold medal in a time of 3:58.8 and Landy the silver in 3:58.9.

They became the first two men to run the mile in less than four minutes in the same race.

Rich Ferguson was third in 4:04.6.

Praising Landy lavishly, Bannister called the last lap of the race the most exciting and intense moment of his life.

"Landy had shown me what a race can really be at its greatest," added Bannister.

"His boldness forced me to abandon my own time schedule and lose myself quite completely in the struggle itself. After this experience I felt I could never again be interested in record-breaking without the thrill of competitive struggle."

23

Gordon Sinclair
Getting into the "Sinc" of things

Gordon Sinclair developed a world-renowned byline in newspaper and magazine adventure writing. He travelled the world as a correspondent, writing about far-away places, wars, monarchs, and all kinds of exotica. It was a colourful, lucrative, enviable lifestyle. But it had its price too.

Between October 1934 and December 1935, Sinclair was home with his wife, Gladys, and their two young sons for just sixteen weeks out of sixty. So early in 1936, after a fallout with the *Toronto Star,* a brief fling with the advertising business, and then a reconciliation with the *Star,* the great Gordon Sinclair tried his hand at sportswriting.

It was a failed effort.

The reason it failed was a lack not of talent, but of patience and tact. The irascible Sinclair specialized in a certain fire-wagon brand of journalism. It was a no-nonsense style that did not leave much room for debate or compromise. His talent lay in writing about what he saw and what he thought about it. Rarely was there anyone able to argue authoritatively with him who had a first-hand experience of his subjects equal to Sinclair's. But, when it came to dealing with Maple Leaf boss Conn Smythe, or writing about baseball, football, rowing and other sports, Sinclair was in over his head.

Once he ran afoul of Conn Smythe and Smythe challenged him to a fight. It seems Sinclair, in one of his columns, had labelled the Leafs "yellow". Smythe confronted Sinclair in a hotel lobby and offered him a room key, suggesting the two go up and slug it out; the one who emerged to come downstairs would win the argument. Sinclair declined but in later years as a hockey fan and a shareholder in Maple Leaf Gardens would sometimes twit Smythe but, for a personal reason, never did more than that.

The personal reason was that one Sunday in New York a few years after the hotel-lobby confrontation, Sinclair had a call from a distraught friend, one of whose relatives had just died in Florida. American money was required to bring the body back to Canada. Sinclair didn't have enough — at the time, under Canadian currency regulations, travellers were allowed a bare minimum for their own needs. Sinclair's New York connections were all in business and publishing. He had no home phone numbers. Then he remembered the Leafs had a game in New York that night. He telephoned Smythe, told him of the dilemma, and Smythe simply growled, "How much do you need?"

That kind of favour, from a man who was by no stretch of the imagination his friend, Sinclair would translate into an indelible mental memo which read: Don't shaft this guy.

Sinclair was off the sports beat after about a year, but he would fence briefly with Conn Smythe once again some twenty years later.

For the 1958-59 season, Sinclair had a press pass good for all events, from opera to wrestling. For hockey games, he had his own subscriber tickets, so he rarely used his press pass or visited the press room on hockey nights. But once he did, and was standing at the free-lunch table eating a small bunch of grapes. Conn Smythe wandered in, saw Sinclair and said loudly, "Sinclair! Are you free-loading again? Ever since you were a kid in Cabbagetown, as long as I've known you, you've been free-loading!"

Sinclair put down the one grape left on his bunch, walked past Smythe and out of the room, his very manner a silent insult.

A day later he was told by the Gardens public relations people that his press pass was being revoked.

His response was to phone his broker and buy ten shares of Maple Leaf Gardens stock, registered in his name.

A week or so later there was another hockey game. Sinclair was there, using his subscriber tickets. Conn Smythe was entertaining guests —

all in dinner jackets, not uncommon at the Gardens in Smythe's heyday. Sinclair, in his usual loud plaid jacket and even louder bow tie, walked up the steps to Smythe's box and told Smythe, also loudly, in front of startled guests, that this or that hockey player was no good and as a shareholder he expected a lot better show than he was getting, continuing to list shortcomings until the puck was dropped. Then he proceeded jauntily to his seat. Mission accomplished.

24

Clarence Campbell
The Richard Riot

During the 1954-55 season Rocket Richard was the most popular player in the province of Quebec, the idol of all French-Canadians and many English-Canadians as well. The Rocket had been the most exciting player of his time and, arguably of all time. He was a voracious goalgetter, frequently carrying two opponents on his back in pursuit of a score. His courage matched his strength but, often, he was attacked by the enemy and, too often, penalties were not called against his assailants.

Usually, Richard would contain the anger he felt against his oppressors but, every so often, he would give vent to it in a verbal explosion which was usually followed by a physical attack against his tormentor. Such was the case on the night of March 13, 1955 at Boston Garden.

Suffering from an already injured back, Richard was further angered when he was struck on the left side of his head by Bruins defenseman Hal Laycoe. Referee Frank Udvari signalled Laycoe to the penalty box but Richard intercepted the Boston player and belabored him about the face and shoulders with his stick. Laycoe survived the blows, dropped his gloves and stick, and beckoned Richard to fight him barehanded.

Linesman Cliff Thompson, a former Boston defenseman, interceded and grabbed Richard's stick away from him. But Richard, now in a frenzy, found another stick and splintered it over Laycoe. This time Laycoe tackled Richard to the ice, but a Montreal player moved in and helped The Rocket to his feet. Richard then charged linesman Thompson, smashing the official until his face was bruised and his eye blackened. More Montreal players intervened and ushered The Rocket to the first-aid room.

Referee Udvari ejected Richard from the game and NHL President Clarence Campbell ordered the scoring ace to his office for a hearing. Normally this would not have been cause for concern in the Canadiens camp — except for two circumstances. On the one hand there was the fact that the regular season was a week from being completed and on the other there was the knowledge throughout the hockey world that, for the first time in his illustrious career, Richard had a grand opportunity to win the NHL scoring championship. At the moment of the Laycoe affair Richard led the league in scoring points.

The consensus among the hockey elite was that Richard could not avoid punishment and that it would take the form of a heavy fine or, at the very worst, suspension for one or two of the remaining games on the schedule. The former would be no problem but the latter would hurt the Rocket's scoring chances and, possibly, deprive him of the title he so desperately coveted. Furthermore, the Canadiens were locked in a neck-and-neck struggle for first place with the hated Detroit Red Wings. Losing Richard, for the Canadiens, would likely mean the loss of first place.

President Campbell was clearly taking all these factors into consideration as he mulled his decision. He had held his hearing with Richard. "I don't remember what happened," he told Campbell. "When I'm hit, I get mad, and I don't know what I do."

Whether Campbell knew what he was doing when he made public his decision is a moot point but the announcement devastated the collective psyche of Quebec like a verbal tornado. "Richard," said Campbell, "is suspended from playing in the remaining league *and* playoff games."

The decision was incredible in its severity and impact on the public at large. "No sports decision ever hit the Montreal public with such impact," commented *Maclean's* magazine. "It seemed to strike at the very heart and soul of the city."

Everywhere people broke down in their own way. Upon hearing the news, a bus driver fell into a daze, ignored a flashing railway crossing signal and almost killed his passengers. The Soviet delegation extended its sympathy to every *Canadien* guest during a social gathering at the Russian embassy in Ottawa.

A man phoned the NHL office and told Campbell's secretary (later his wife) Phyllis King that he was an undertaker. "Tell him," the voice said, "that he'll be needing me in a few days."

Another caller threatened to assassinate Campbell. "I'm no crank," he added, "but I'm going to blow your place up."

The French-Canadian press fanned the flames of passion with incendiary editorials. "If The Rocket's name was Richardson," wrote one French-Canadian fan, "you would have given a different verdict."

Montreal's French-Canadian Mayor Jean Drapeau added: "It would not be necessary to give too many such decisions to kill hockey in Montreal."

Making matters worse was the knowledge among every hockey fan that the Canadiens very next game, on Thursday, March 17th would be against the Detroit Red Wings at the Forum. Facing the vaunted Detroit club led by Gordie Howe and Ted Lindsay would be difficult without Richard. The fans, filled with fury, marched down Ste. Catherine Street to the Forum. Some carried signs, "*Vive* Richard" and "*A Bas* Campbell."

Aware that NHL President Campbell attended virtually every home game of the Canadiens — his office was in Montreal — the police hoped that he would exercise discretion and remain home on this sensitive occasion. But Campbell declared that he had no intentions of missing the game. "I'm a season ticket-holder," he said, "and a regular attendant, and I have a right to go. I felt that the police could protect me."

Campbell, of course, was being naive. Given the configuration of the Forum, it would have been difficult, if not impossible, to station enough *gendarmes* in an arena filled with more than 13,000 fans around him to ensure his physical safety.

The opening face-off, as always, would take place at 8:30 p.m. By that time there were more than 600 militant demonstrators gathered on Ste. Catherine Street West in front of the Forum and on Atwater and Closse Streets, which bound the side entrances.

Campbell, who had dined at the Montreal Amateur Athletic Association, was delayed by the meal and arrived at the garage two blocks east of the Forum later than he had anticipated. Campbell found a policeman and asked to be escorted to his seat. They walked to his box at the south end of the rink and Campbell took his seat.

By this time the crowd, even without Campbell's appearance, was in an ugly mood. Playing without their leader Richard, the Canadiens were disorganized and fell behind, 2-1, to the Red Wings.

The late appearance of Campbell, after nearly all of the other spectators had taken their seats, merely magnified his presence and made him an even greater target than he might have been had he appeared more discreetly. The fans chanted anti-Campbell slogans in French and English and increased their intensity as the Canadiens fell behind, 4-1.

As the intermission approached, a torrent of debris poured down upon the NHL president and his guests. His secretary, Phyllis King, was wearing a white straw hat which was knocked off her head by a flying rubber boot. A bunch of assorted fruit defaced Campbell's green fedora but most of the missiles flew wide of the target. To pin-point the president, one anti-Campbell spectator rose in his seat and directed the fire of those above him. When a soda pop bottle struck a woman nearby, several fans implored Campbell to leave, but the implacable president remained seated and even managed to force a smile.

"I tried to avoid doing anything that would provoke the crowd," said Campbell. Nevertheless, a youngster swooped down from above and punched Campbell about the face. Police rushed in and ushered the fan away but that was only the beginning of Campbell's troubles. As the siren wailed, signalling the end of the first period dozens of spectators charged

48

Campbell's seat and his party was completely encircled by a mob which observers contend was bent on killing the president.

Maclean's reported: "The ill-feeling was growing more intense by the second, and there was nobody to help him. Looking around at the sea of hate-filled faces, Miss King had the feeling they were closing in for the kill."

Campbell didn't know it at the time but a few seconds later an explosion would rock the ancient arena — and thereby save his life. An unidentified fan hurled a tear gas cannister which landed 25 feet from Campbell and instantly distracted those who were after his scalp. Within seconds the cry of "fire" was heard in every section of the building until onlookers began choking and rubbing their eyes and throats.

Seizing Miss King by the arm, Campbell headed directly to the Forum first-aid room where he conferred with Fire Commissioner Armand Pare and the Canadiens managing director Frank Selke. Campbell then dispatched a note to Red Wings manager Jack Adams: "The game has been forfeited to Detroit. You are entitled to take your team on its way anytime now. Selke agrees as the fire department has ordered the building closed."

By 11 p.m. the mob outside the Forum had swollen to at least 10,000, each of whom wanted a piece of Campbell. The league president remained in the first-aid room, still relatively poised, considering the circumstances. "I never was afraid of being lynched," he insisted. "As a referee, I learned something about mobs. They're cowards."

Just before midnight, Jim Hunter, the Forum building superintendent, and a burly constable led Campbell and Miss King to Hunter's car in the back of the Forum. They drove the president home, and as soon as he reached his apartment he phoned his father in Edmonton to assure him he was safe.

L'affaire Richard was not over. The crowd in front of the Forum turned into a rioting band of looters who smashed store windows up and down Ste. Catherine Street. By early morning, when the rioters were finally dispersed, police had arrested 70 people and counted 50 stores damaged or looted.

Mayor Drapeau said the riots occurred because of "provocation caused by Campbell's presence." To that the president replied: "Does he think I should have yielded to the intimidation of a bunch of hoodlums?"

In the afternoon Richard drove down to the Forum where he delivered a public address in French to the press, pleading for law and order. "I would like to ask everyone to get behind the team and help the boys win from the Rangers and Detroit."

The Canadiens could not fulfill the entire request. They beat the Rangers but lost to Detroit and finished in second place. The suspension also cost Rocket Richard the scoring championship. Teammate Bernie Geoffrion outpointed Richard and took the title away from him. Detroit completed the humiliation by defeating Montreal in the Stanley Cup finals. As for Campbell, he survived demands that he resign and remained NHL president until 1977.

25

Chuck Ryan
Flight of the Bumble Skis

For ski jumpers, it's always "Look, Ma, no hands!" For ski jumper Chuck Ryan at the 1959 Duluth Invitational, it was "Look, Ma, no skis!"

More than 2,500 fans were on hand that day in Fond du Lac, Minnesota for the ski jumping championships. They were hoping to see at least one record jump. Ryan hadn't planned on it, but he set the unofficial record for the longest jump without skis.

Ryan, a nine-year veteran with the St. Paul Ski Club, should have brought a parachute before starting down the sixty-metre ramp, because when he hit the takeoff point, both his skis flew off his feet! Soaring through the air for 150 feet, Ryan cursed himself for using a new set of skis without testing the bindings. Then he told himself to prepare for a rough landing. He hit the snow at an angle and skidded about another 100 feet before coming to a stop, unhurt.

"I just jumped out of my skis," said the 26-year-old skier.

"I wasn't really scared, but I kept thinking that I better not land on my feet and risk breaking my legs. So I went in like a baseball player sliding into second."

26

Muhammad Ali / Cassius Clay
All that glitters...

Cassius Marcellus Clay Jr. was born in Louisville, Kentucky, January 17, 1942. A poor kid, he took up boxing when he was 12, fighting for six years as an amateur, winning 100 of his 108 matches.

In 1960, he exploded onto the U.S. sports scene, dazzling fight fans with a showy style, fancy footwork and superb boxing skills that won him a gold medal in the Olympics in Rome.

That gold medal was destined for the bottom of the Ohio River.

After the win in Rome, Clay was welcomed back to the U.S. with much acclaim. But even the Olympic gold medalist could not avoid the social realities of the American South in 1960.

Cassius Clay, the returning hero, was refused service in a restaurant in his hometown of Louisville ... because he was black.

Clay went directly from the restaurant to a nearby bridge over the Ohio River, angrily took the medal he had been proudly wearing around his neck, and threw it into the water.

Clay, of course, eventually got over the pain of that experience. A few months later, in October of 1960, he won his first professional bout. Three and a half years later, on February 25, 1964, Clay beat the heavy-

51

weight champion, Sonny Liston, in the seventh round of a scheduled 15-round title fight.

The next day, the new champ announced that he had become a Black Muslim and changed his name to Muhammad Ali. He went on to become what most agree was the greatest heavyweight champ ever, winning the title an unprecedented three separate times.

27

The 1960 World Series
Mazerozki's Moment

The 1960 World Series was a wacky one. The Pirates and the Yankees provided plenty of excitement, but offered no pattern for predictions on how it would turn out. The Pirates were winners in the first game, and were then slaughtered in the next two, but fought back with two more successive victories. Yankee power asserted itself in game six and then the Pirates used the Bronx Bombers' own weapon, the long ball, to triumph in game 7.

It was Thursday, October 13th, at Pittsburgh. The series was tied 3-games each. The Yankee wins had been convincing ones; 16-3, 10-0 and 12-0. The Pirates had scratched out 6-4, 3-2 and 5-2 victories.

The Yanks had Mantle, Maris, Skowron and Richardson crushing the ball; in fact, their batting order sported a .338 average in the series, the highest ever in World Series play. They also had Whitey Ford spinning some pitching gems on the mound.

Still, the Pirates had hung in and the series went to a seventh game.

In the final game the Yanks were hitting the ball as hard as ever, but it was Pittsburgh that took a four run lead early on. Rocky Nelson's two run homer brought home a couple, then Bill Virdon poked a single, scoring men from second and third.

The Yankees strained at the leash a bit when Moose Skowron drove a ball into the seats in their fifth. Next inning, the Yankees got two men aboard with a single and a walk and it was time for another appearance from Pirate reliever, Elroy Face. But he was shaky, giving up a single to Mantle and a home run to Berra. Face got out of the sixth, through the seventh and then into trouble again in the eighth, as Skowron, Blanchard and Boyer all hit safely, making the score 7-4 Yankees.

The Pirates pinch-hit for Face next inning, and Gino Cimoli poked a single. Next up, Bill Virdon hit a ball that, as it turned out, cost the ballgame for New York. The ball skipped sharply to Tony Kubek at short for what looked to be an easy double play. But just as it reached him, it hit a pebble, or a hard spot and took a sudden wild bound. The ball struck Kubek in the Adam's apple and sent him crumpling to the ground. Cimoli was safe at second and Virdon at first; Kubek had to leave the game. After that, two more singles and a homer by the Pirates gave them five runs in the inning and a 9-7 lead.

The Yankees got back into it with two more in the top of the ninth on singles by Richardson, by pinch-hitter Dale Long and by Mantle.

So, 9-9 in the bottom of the ninth of the seventh game of the World Series, as the "weak end" of the order was due up, Bill Mazerozki stepped in to open the home half of the inning. He watched the first pitch go by. The second came in a little higher and it suited him just right. With a clean, easy swing he met it head on and sent the ball sailing over the scoreboard, where the score read 9-9. The Mazerozki homer changed that to 10-9 and the Pirates were champions.

The crowd broke loose then and some of them trotted down the third base-line with Maz. The celebration in Pittsburgh lasted all night, filling the streets with torn-up paper, unearthly noise, stalled trolleys, dancing fans of all ages, weary policemen and bewildered dogs and cats.

Bobby Richardson
Priorities

In this day of the multi-million dollar athlete, signing bonuses, free agency, contract holdouts and the like, can there be a more amazing and refreshing story than that of Bobby Richardson, the great second baseman for the Yankees in the late 50's and early 60's.

A deeply religious man from South Carolina with a strong sense of family, Richardson decided when he was just 30 that he had played his last game. He was leaving to spend more time with his wife and children.

The Yankees owner, Del Webb, knew that Richardson's departure would leave a big gap at second (some say the Yankee infield in 1961, with Moose Skowron at first, Richardson at second, Kubek at short and Clete Boyer at third, was the best ever) so he thought he'd try to change Richardson's mind with a big money offer.

Webb offered Richardson a blank contract, asking him to fill in the salary numbers.

Richardson pushed the blank contract back across the table saying, "The Yankees have treated me well, and I am not interested in filling in the blanks on that contract. I am interested in filling in the blanks in my life as a husband and a father. My last game was my last game."

An incredulous Webb said later, "I was doing my job. The team needed him. He was only 30 and the Yankees would be a better team with him at second. I had to try to keep him. I was running a business, but he was running his life. Bobby never tried to convince any of us we should believe as he did, but we all knew how he felt. After that I really knew what he was made of."

29

Goaltenders
A Breed Apart

Hockey goaltenders have always had the reputation of being a special breed. Perhaps the most famous for his eccentricities and innovations was Jacques Plante, six time Vezina trophy winner with the Canadiens in the late 50's, but even more renowned as the first NHL goalie to wear a mask and to make a habit of playing the puck behind the net. Less well-known, perhaps, is the story of Plante and the Chicago net. When the great goalie kept complaining that he was always bumping into the cross-bar of one of the nets at the Chicago Stadium, no one took much notice. But Plante was nothing if not strong-willed, and he eventually insisted on having the net measured. Sure enough, it was inches short of the regulation four-foot height.

Glenn Hall, a contemporary of Plante's, was almost as important an innovator; his technique of dropping to his knees, pads spread along the ice to either side, has been picked up by almost every professional goalie since as a useful method of improving one's save percentage on screened shots. Hall once described to journalist Stan Fischler his feelings about the game: "It's stimulating and rewarding, but it can tear you apart. Before every game, and sometimes between periods, I get sick to my stomach; I have to throw up. Sometimes it happens during a game. When that happens, I fight it off until the whistle blows. Then I head for the dressing room. I've tried drinking tea between periods and that seems to help. But I don't worry about it because nervousness is a part of this game and, in its way, it helps keep you sharp."

Another great goalie who often experienced the same symptoms was

Gump Worsley. For Worsley, though, the worst nervousness was not in the net (he was one of the last bare-headed NHL goalies) but in the air. So petrified was he of flying that for a time he would take the train on road trips while the rest of the Canadiens flew. The lovable Worsley also delivered one of hockey's classic quips. Before being traded it was the Gumper's fate to toil for the New York Rangers. In the late 1950's and early 1960's the Rangers almost always finished fifth or sixth — in a six-team league. In the midst of one interview with Worsley a journalist made the mistake of asking Gump which NHL team gave him the most trouble. Worsley didn't have to think long before answering the question: "the Rangers".

30

Sam Snead
The Presidential Pro

Sam Snead is a golf legend.

He won twenty-six PGA tournaments in his career, pretty much owning the links in the 1940's and 50's. By independent records he has 135 career victories, 165 by his own count.

He is the only man to have won PGA golf tournaments in six different decades!

He is also a heckuva storyteller, and one with a typical reverence for the U.S. presidency ... even on the golf course, even when the play is less than impressive.

Having played golf with Presidents Eisenhower and Nixon, Snead was in a position to evaluate their games.

Ike was a great guy. He loved his golf and he loved playing with me. He always told everyone around him to call him "Ike", but with my time in the service I couldn't help but think of him as the Commander-in-Chief and could never bring myself to call him "Ike" in person.

Ike never asked for tips, he had his own game. Once when we played in Washington, he wasn't doing very well. He had those little glasses, and if he turned his head just a little, he wouldn't be looking out of those glasses anymore but out the side.

He also had a short backswing that was causing him to lose power on his drives. The problem was so obvious I didn't hesitate to give him my advice: "You've got to stick your butt out more, Mr. President."

His bodyguards couldn't believe I'd said that to the President of the United States. Neither could I, but Ike was too intent on his game to notice.

I thought about his glasses problem, and when I next played with him and he had his doctor with him I said to the doctor, "Why don't you get him some of those wraparound eyeglasses, so then he can turn as much as he wants to?"

He did and it worked for Ike, and in appreciation he gave me three of his golf balls, autographed by him. I still have them.

When I look at those presidential golf balls I also remember that, after the business of the glasses, I started seeing Ike playing golf in − what else? − a palmetto hat with a wide band, just like mine.

Nixon wasn't the player Ike was − never scored as low, though he played pretty often. When he was Ike's number two man he couldn't break 100. He was dying to give Ike a game, so I advised him to use his wedge more until he felt he had greater control over pitches and chips. Soon he was down into the 80's.

Once, I played for two weeks with Nixon down at Greenbrier in West Virginia, and he was good company. Yes, I liked him, and I think he made a hell of a President. He got caught doing something petty that he shouldn't have done, but it shouldn't have made people overlook all the good things. So speaks Sam Snead, golfer-politician. But, hell, even a golfer has a right to his opinions.

To tell you the truth though, I did catch Nixon once myself.

He'd landed in some rough no one could shoot out of unless you had a bazooka. I was watching him from the fairway when he disappeared into a thicket. Hell, I figured he was going to drop another ball, take his loss like anyone else in that situation and play on. But, hell no — out comes his ball flyin' high onto the fairway. Then Nixon comes out of the woods looking real pleased with himself. I knew he threw it out, but I didn't say anything.

What could I say? He was the President.

31

Gene Conley
Proposed Pilgrimage

Although he had a fine career with the Boston Red Sox and the Boston Braves, pitcher Gene Conley may be remembered best for a strange sequence of events in 1962 when he actually went AWOL and bought a plane ticket to Israel to "get nearer to God."

Conley was going through a bad stretch with the Red Sox, and like any pitcher on a bad ball club, was losing ballgames due to non-support. He had gone 23 innings without his teammates having scored a run for him.

Conley was on the mound pitching against the Yankees in July when they erupted for eight runs in the third inning to chase him.

On the bus back to the airport, Conley had time to think about the season. After a while he decided he and teammate E.J. "Pumpsie" Green would go carousing while his teammates travelled back to Boston.

After a few scotches, Conley tried to convince Green to fly to Israel with him.

"I had started reading the Bible about that time. The more I got tanked, the more it made sense to me. 'Hey,' I thought. 'I'm going to Bethlehem and Jerusalem and get all my problems straightened out and come back a big winner.'"

As it turned out, Green didn't go with Conley, but Conley tried to go anyway. He bought his ticket but was refused passage because he didn't have a passport. He went instead to Providence on a bender and surfaced a few days later in Boston.

Maybe the pilgrimage to Israel was a wild idea, but Conley went on to have his best year, winning fifteen games.

32

Grey Cup, 1962
From the Shores of Lake Erie

Few CFL fans above a certain age will forget the 1962 Grey Cup game at CNE Stadium in Toronto. Those who watched it, either live or on television, could see little except shadows darting in and out of the ever-thickening fog. With 9:29 remaining, the game was finally halted, and the Winnipeg Blue Bombers had to wait until the next day to try to hold their 28-27 lead over the Hamilton Tiger-Cats. Oddly, the teams were unable to score in normal visibility, and the Bombers eventually captured the Cup.

The Game gave rise to hundreds of anecdotes. One of the more amusing concerns then-Prime Minister John Diefenbaker, who was caught in a particularly thick wave of fog as he took a break from the action. He was halfway through the door before he (or his aides) realized it was the ladies' rather than the men's room.

The game was also the first Grey Cup to be shown on American national television — or at least that was the plan. The fog delay forced Johnny Esaw and his crew to scramble frantically to provide season high-lights to fill the space. But it is doubtful whether or not the fog should be blamed for the ABC crew signing off from Toronto with the words, "That's all from the shores of Lake Erie."

33

Harry Jerome
Silencing the Critics

He ran like the wind, but often it seemed to be an ill wind that was blowing when Canadian sprinter Harry Jerome laced on a pair of track shoes.

A sprinting legend, Jerome was the only man ever to hold the world records in the 100-metre and the 100-yard dash at the same time. He won an Olympic bronze medal and a gold in the British Empire Games and was a world-class sprinter for the better part of a decade. But there were times in that decade when there were injuries and bitter failures, and harsh criticism from the press.

Jerome was born on July 15, 1940 in Prince Albert, Saskatchewan, the fourth of five children. His father was a porter on the railroad; his grandfather an Olympic sprinter. Jerome was a nineteen-year old University of Oregon student when he stunned observers at the 1960 Canadian Olympic trials in Saskatoon by running the 100-metres in ten seconds flat, thereby tying the world record set less than a month earlier by Armin Hary of West Germany.

That won Jerome a trip to the 1960 Olympics in Rome, where he began by breaking the 100-metre Olympic record of 10.3 seconds during the heats, but suffered a muscle injury in the semi-finals and was forced to the sidelines. Two years later, he held a share of the world record for the 100-yard dash at 9.2 seconds, but again succumbed to an injury during the British Empire Games in Perth, Australia. This time he had an infected throat, later diagnosed as tonsilitis, and a leg injury that threatened his career.

The press was unforgiving when Jerome pulled up lame in Perth, hinting that he folded up in the big races. "Jerome's shocking humiliation when he finished dead last in the British Empire Games 100-yard dash final clouded what could have been Canada's finest hour in big-time international competition since the war," wrote Jack Sullivan of the Canadian Press.

The leg injury forced Jerome to spend months in hospital and then on crutches. Doctors believed he might never run again, but he returned to make the Canadian sprint team that was to go to the 1964 Olympics in Tokyo. He made the Canadian squad with a controversial performance at the Canadian Olympic trials in St. Lambert, Quebec. "He refused to try for good times, ran the heats and the semifinals from a standing start, wearing sweatpants and sunglasses," one Toronto newspaper noted.

But he went on to win the bronze medal in the 100-metre final at the Olympics and he came fourth in the 200-metre. Jerome followed that performance up with a gold medal in the 100-yard at the 1966 British Empire Games in Kingston, Jamaica, the same year he ran the 100-yard in 9.1 seconds. "Nobody yelled 'quitter' this time," wrote Sullivan.

Jerome returned in 1968 for his third Olympics, came seventh in the 100-metre final and retired that year. He moved into sports administration, both provincially and federally. Many of the programs he developed are still in place, including plans to promote fitness at the elementary school level. He also cajoled various levels of government to improve their minority rights programs.

Harry Jerome was forty-two years old when he died of a brain seizure in 1982.

In addition to his great talent on the track, Harry Jerome stands as a model of resilience and fortitude. He bounced back and defied the writers and track officials who had expected and, indeed, demanded so much of him in the early 60's. They were on his bandwagon when he was a prodigy in the early 60's but were merciless in their criticism when he faltered in Rome in 1960 and Perth in 1962. In the end, in spite of them all, Harry Jerome was a success, and he achieved it alone.

34

Yogi Berra
The Quotes

It's unfortunate that Yogi Berra is more often remembered for his strange sayings rather than for his prowess as a baseball player.

Yogi was a great player. He's in the Hall of Fame. His lifetime batting average was .285. But former teammates say it's a shame they don't keep records the way they do now, because if they did, they'd find that in the seventh, eighth and ninth innings, with men on base, Yogi Berra must have hit about .400.

Still, it is the quotes attributed to him that make Yogi the stuff of baseball stories. Here are a few of the choice ones, some of which Yogi can explain...

"It ain't over 'till it's over."

Is it the best thing I've ever said? I hope not. (And I try to say: "it ISN'T over 'till it's over." I said it in 1973. The way the Mets were bouncing around in the standings that year, it was true. We won the National League division by winning 82 games and losing 79. That was a 50.9% average, and I meant it isn't over until a team is in first place after the last game. Sometimes it's over before it begins — if I fought Joe Louis in his prime, it would be over before it began.

When I was watching an old Steve McQueen movie on TV, I said, "Oh, he must have made that before he died." I said that about Jeff Chandler and some other actors too. Seemed to make sense at the time.

When I went to the Mayor's mansion in New York City on a hot day, Mayor Lindsay's wife, Mary, said to me, "You look nice and cool, Yogi." I answered, "You don't look so hot yourself." I didn't mean for it to sound that way, and Mrs. Lindsay knew what I meant.

A bunch of reporters were asking me questions one day, trying to get me to say something they could write about. One question was, "What would you do if you found a million dollars?" I said, "If the guy was poor, I would give it back." Seems dumb now, but it made sense to me at the time I thought of it.

Bunch of the guys on the team one time were bored and wanted to go see a dirty movie. I said "no" over and over, but they kept bugging me, so I said, "Okay, who's in it?" People seem to think that response is great, and it may be. I'm just happy they know I don't like going to dirty movies.

"Baseball is 90 percent mental; the other half is physical." This is always accompanied by a writer saying, "Yogi may think fine, but he can't add." I still think anybody who plays golf or tennis or any other sport knows what I mean.

President Bush is a baseball fan. He played first base for Yale. When he was vice-president, he was campaigning through Texas and was on hand to throw out the first ball at an Astros' game. I got to meet him and we discussed politics a bit. He said, "Yogi, Texas is very important." I said, "I know, Texas has a lot of electrical votes." He didn't smile, because he knew what I meant.

Once when a waitress asked if I wanted my pizza cut into eight slices or four, I said, "Four, I don't think I can eat eight." Right after I said it, I knew she was going to laugh and write it down. I was with my son, Tim. He knew what I meant, but I know that she didn't.

Enos Slaughter and Joe Page went hunting once and Joe said Enos had been jumping in and out of the bushes so much looking for quail that he got a cyst on his back. I don't hunt, so I thought it was a pretty innocent question when I asked, "What kind of bird is a cyst?" People have asked dumber questions. Lots dumber.

My wife, Carmen, tells one that I find funny. It's about Venetian blinds. We were going to have some of ours repaired only I didn't know it. I was upstairs when our son, Larry, called out, "Dad, the man is here for the Venetian blinds." I told him to look in my pants pocket and give them a five dollar donation.

63

Once when I bought some life insurance, I was getting some heat from one of the guys in the clubhouse. He said I was wasting my money and what good would it do me. I got mad and said "I'll get it when I die." I didn't understand as much about insurance as I should, but I understood that as a young father I should have some.

Some of the things they said I said, I didn't.

"Never answer an anonymous letter." I didn't say it, but, it sounds like good advice.

It's not me but a friend of mine who calls those low-slung German dogs, "Datsuns."

There is a dog and car story that has come back to haunt me though. A friend of mine never lets me forget it. He came to our house one day with a big dog in the back of his car. He said, "What do you think of my daughter's Afghan?" I said, "Looks nice; I'm thinking about getting a Chevy Vega."

There are others that people still get a kick out of. I did call Joe Altobelli an "Italian Scallion."

When I was in spring training once, an equipment manager asked me what size cap I wore. I did respond, "I don't know, I'm not in shape yet."

I did say, "a dime isn't worth a nickel anymore." It's not.

But I didn't say, "It's deja vu all over again."

Nor did I say, "Always go to other people's funerals or they won't come to yours."

By the time Johnny Bench broke my record for most home runs by a catcher, I had the reputation I have now. Someone sent him a telegram saying, "Congratulations. I knew the record would stand only 'til it was broken." I don't know who sent it, but it was signed, Yogi Berra.

The story goes that I went to see a sportswriter once and said, "I went three-for-four yesterday and your paper said I was two-for-four." The writer is supposed to have said, "It was a typographical error." I'm supposed to have said, "Like hell it was. It was a clean single to right." Nice story. It never happened.

One I'm proud of is, "You can see a lot by just observing." It's the way I felt when I said it. I don't know when that was. I think I would say it the same way today.

Yogi Berra had a way with words to be sure. Some of his sayings and purported sayings are ridiculous. But, some are quite simple and straight-forward and perhaps we just didn't listen hard enough.

My favorite, and one to which many of us can no doubt relate, is Yogi's now-famous theory on a certain popular restaurant.

"No wonder no one goes there anymore; it's always too crowded."
Makes sense to me.

35

Harold Ballard
Bullying even the Beatles

Harold Ballard, with his partners, Stafford Smythe and John Bassett, took over the operation of the Toronto Maple Leafs and of their building, Maple Leaf Gardens in 1961. Initially, the hockey operation was left to Stafford Smythe, whose father, Conn, had built the arena and the hockey team back in the early 1930's and had run both for years.

With Stafford Smythe becoming president and running the hockey end of things, the sharp-minded businessman, Ballard, took over as executive vice-president in charge of running the arena. Bassett was named Chairman of the Board. Ballard was always number three in the pecking order of this triumvirate. Smythe was the patriarch's son, the heir and kingpin of the organization. Bassett was the playboy-sportsman type, also involved with the pro football franchise in Toronto, the Argonauts, and was active in politics with the Progressive Conservatives.

With these three in charge of things, the operation was about to enter a golden era, a time of unprecedented prosperity, glamour and excitement. On the ice, the Leafs would win four Stanley Cups. The Gardens would become a multi-purpose entertainment mecca and a huge money-maker.

Once, in the fall of 1962, Ballard tried to swing a hockey deal to send the Leafs' star left-winger at that time, Frank Mahovlich, to Chicago for $1 million. Ballard felt he and his partners could use the money to lighten their debt load. But, in the end, the deal was quashed by Stafford Smythe.

For years after that, Ballard kept right out of the hockey affairs and, instead, devoted all his energy to increasing the profits of Maple Leaf Gardens.

He quickly negotiated a new TV contract for Leaf games, increasing the annual fee to about $700,000. In 1965, he secured a six-year, $9 million deal with MacLaren Advertising for radio and television rights plus exploitation of the Gardens premises for advertising. He introduced advertising to the Gardens, something old Conn Smythe found crassly commercial.

For Smythe, that was not the worst of it. He considered another of Ballard's early acts almost treasonous — the removal of a large portrait of Queen Elizabeth II, which had dominated one end of the Gardens during Smythe's regime. The portrait was thrown out to make room for more seats, a decision which enraged monarchists. "If people want to see a picture of the Queen, they can go to an art gallery," said Ballard. "She doesn't pay me ... and besides, what position can a Queen play?"

Nor, for that matter did she buy advertising space at the Gardens, but C-C-M did, paying about $15,000 a year for signs at each end of the rink. The Ford people did the same. Ads for Schick razor blades could be found on the escalator risers, and even on the bottoms of the seats. Soon, the space on the ice-flooding machine was sold to Dominion Stores and the Gardens program was revamped with more advertising.

The ads, the television deals, the concessions, the larger number and smaller-sized seats all helped, but the big money came from simply using the Gardens more often for more attractions. During Conn Smythe's time, almost all the arena revenue came from NHL hockey, junior hockey, a few circuses and a few ice shows. There would be the occasional political convention or religious meeting, but that was the extent of it.

Ballard changed all this by bringing in concerts and entertainment acts.

At first, this was not largely successful. Case in point; in 1963, the Tommy Dorsey Band was booked and only drew 1,000 people and poor reviews. But, by the mid-to-late sixties, rock concerts were extremely popular and Ballard had them at the Gardens on a regular basis. In 1965, the Gardens had twenty-one more nights of entertainment than it had had the previous year. Similar increases followed in 1966 and again in 1967.

The beginning may have been in 1964, with the Beatles. Ballard booked them for September 7th, and the concert was hyped to the hilt. There were mob scenes and teenaged girls fainting and crowds screaming. Not much music could be heard, but the concert was judged a success. In the summer of 1965, the Beatles made their second trip to Toronto. This was the occasion when Ballard pulled one of his most devious stunts.

With fans lining up for blocks to get tickets weeks before, Ballard decided to sell tickets for two shows, even though the Beatles itinerary only planned for one. When the Beatles arrived from their memorable Shea Stadium concert in New York, their manager, Brian Epstein, was furious to find Ballard promoting TWO sold-out shows.

A Gardens employee remembers, "Epstein was in Ballard's office yelling his head off."

"Look, the tickets are sold. If you don't go on, they'll tear this place down and you with it," Ballard retorted.

Then Ballard told his employee, to "take this guy down to the Hot Stove Lounge (the Gardens pub) and get him stiff."

It was one of the hottest days of the summer, and more than 300 fans fainted from the heat and hysteria as 18,000 jammed the Gardens for each performance. It was then that another Ballard scheme went into effect.

Ballard purposely delayed each performance, the first by 75 minutes, the second by 90 minutes. During that time he had the Gardens workers turn off the air-conditioning, turn on the heat, shut off the fountains, and told the concession staff to put away all the small soft drink cups. By selling the large soft drinks to the thirsty concert fans, large profits were made. The Beatles did well too, earning $100,000 instead of $50,000.

Since then, Ballard has gone to jail for tax evasion, taken over full control of the Gardens and the hockey club, battled against admitting the WHA teams in the late 70's, has publicly embarrassed players, drummed popular men like Keon, Sittler, MacDonald, Williams, and Vaive out of Toronto, and has generally meddled in his team's hockey affairs to the point where the Leafs are now one of the league doormats, and have not won a Stanley Cup in more than two decades.

36

Dorothy Cavis-Brown
Tired of Tennis

Imagine waking up from a nice snooze, stretching and expecting to see the light streaming in from your bedroom window. Instead you bolt up and, with a sickening feeling in the pit of your stomach, you realize you're on a tennis court at Wimbledon where two tennis players and thousands of fans are laughing at you.

Such an incredibly embarrassing moment befell Dorothy Cavis-Brown, a lineswoman who actually fell asleep in – of all places – the middle of a 1964 match at the oldest and most prestigious tennis tournament in the world.

Dorothy, one of the most respected lineswomen in England at the time, was responsible for watching one of the sidelines during a match between American Clark Graebner and South African Abe Segal. Staring at a line got so boring that she fell asleep on the job in the final set. At first, all eyes were on the tennis action; no one noticed the prim and proper Englishwoman as she dozed and tilted to one side in her chair.

Graebner, who wound up losing in straight sets, didn't realize the lineswoman was slumbering until Segal hit a shot wide of the line and Dorothy didn't call it "out." In fact, Dorothy didn't call it anything. Instead of 40-love, it was 40 winks!

"I noticed that she was slumped over slightly, head down," Graebner recalled.

"I went over and nudged her. Frankly it was to see if she had died. Well, she bobbed her head slightly, but she didn't wake up. Eventually she did, but by then everyone had noticed her dozing. In the stands there was quite a lot of uproarious laughter, at least by British standards."

Chagrined officials at the All England Club decided it was best if Dorothy took a couple of days off from the tournament to catch up on her sleep. She was rarely seen at the club again.

Some said Dorothy was spending most of her time in the land of Nod.

37

Danny Gallivan
We interrupt this broadcast...

Hockey play-by-play legend Danny Gallivan was, for years, one of the great voices of television's *Hockey Night in Canada*. With the years of calling the Montreal Canadiens games from the broadcast booth at the Forum, it was natural that certain routines and habits would emerge as part of Gallivan's delivery. While phrases like "canonading drive," "spinarama move," and, "caught up in his paraphernalia" became his signature, he also had a habit that went on longer than it needed to. In the old days, Gallivan used a hand-held microphone much like a stage-singer would. Later, as technology developed, *Hockey Night in Canada* switched to headsets with microphones attached, alleviating the need for the hands to be occupied. Still, Gallivan was so used to the old hand-held style that he was seen in the Forum press box on occasion using a pencil as a surrogate microphone, even when he was just looking on as a spectator and not doing the play-by-play. When broadcasting, Gallivan, for a time, persisted in holding a "dead" or unconnected microphone in his hand while his call of the action was actually going through the headset apparatus. One night, when he felt a frog in his throat, he leaned on an old habit of holding his microphone far away from him, covering it somewhat with his other hand and simply clearing his throat with an unabashed gutteral grunt. He had forgotten of course that he was wearing the headset microphone and every ear-curdling movement of his saliva and throat juices went out coast to coast.

38

Northern Dancer
With the Look of Eagles

On the afternoon of Monday, February 24, 1964, veteran Canadian sportswriter, Jim Coleman, sat at a typewriter in the pressbox at Hialeah Park in Florida, tingling with excitement as he wrote of an extraordinary performance he had just witnessed:

"A bull-chested colt sped through the sun drenched homestretch at Hialeah today and rushed toward the threshold of equine immortality.

"You can paste this warning in your hatband right now and refer to it on the afternoon of Saturday, May 2nd: Northern Dancer will be the first Canadian-bred to win the Kentucky Derby."

Northern Dancer's greatest achievements still lay ahead of him when those words were written, but Coleman made no claim to unusual prescience. He said any man with an eye for equine grandeur would have discerned, immediately, that Northern Dancer was one of those rare super-horses "with the look of eagles."

In the thoroughbred horse establishment which E.P. Taylor was operating in 1960, matings of expensive sires and mares were planned very carefully by Taylor and his bloodstock advisers. However, the mating which produced Northern Dancer was not one embarked upon after careful study of bloodlines, omens and auguries. Northern Dancer resulted from a "marriage of expedience": the mating of an unproven stallion named Nearctic and a very young mare named Natalma.

Nearctic was a good horse but not a great horse. He did set Canadian records for five furlongs and for six furlongs and did win the Michigan Mile in track-record time in July of 1958. Taylor picked up a purse cheque for $40,000. He later used $30,000 of that money to buy a bay filly named Natalma, sired by the great grey race horse Native Dancer.

Natalma appeared destined for racing distinction, but never quite made it. In all, she won three of her seven starts and, as a three-year-old, went to Churchill Downs as a prospective favorite for the Kentucky Oaks. A week before that important engagement, she broke a knee-bone.

Taylor called an emergency meeting in Toronto to discuss the horse's future. One alternative he talked about with his people was to send the filly to the University of Pennsylvania where veterinarians were experimenting with a new type of surgery for knee fractures. The other alternative was to breed Natalma, although she was only a three-year-old.

And what Taylor stud was immediately available? Well, there was Nearctic. It was strictly a gamble — Nearctic was standing his first season on the farm and there was no way of telling if he would sire good horses or bad horses. So that's the way it was to be: Nearctic and Natalma. So much for scientific matings, carefully planned by equine-breeding pundits!

Natalma was delivered of her foal on May 21, 1961. At first, the Taylor people were enthused, calling Northern Dancer "the best looking yearling we've ever had." Twelve months later though, they changed their tune. Northern Dancer hadn't grown as tall as his fellow yearlings. He was called "short and chunky" and was put up for sale in September of 1962 for the price of $25,000.

No one bought him.

At Taylor's annual sale, where astute horsemen appraised and inspected the yearlings up for sale, Northern Dancer was passed over for taller, flashier colts.

One of the best bargains in the history of Canadian horse racing had slipped through the fingers of dozens of potential buyers.

The Dancer stayed in the home-barn for training with the other horses in Taylor's Canadian division and was brought along slowly because he was a "late foal" and was undersized. He didn't make his debut under the silks until August 2nd of his two-year-old season, at Fort Erie. He won his first start and had a series of good finishes there, in Toronto, and, later, in New York.

After reparations were made to a cracked hoof, Northern Dancer was shipped to Florida in 1964 to prepare for his date with destiny.

On that sunny afternoon at Hialeah, the Dancer was running in an old-fashioned sporting trial — a race with no purse and no betting. The race itself proved to be no contest. Northern Dancer simply ran away and hid on his two rivals. The Canadian bandwagon picked up a fresh load of converts as it rolled on toward Kentucky.

The world's most successful jockey, Bill Shoemaker, rode the Dancer in that sporting trial at Hialeah and later won the Flamingo Stakes and the Florida Derby aboard the stocky Canadian colt. There was an informal understanding that he would be in the irons for the Kentucky Derby too.

But "The Shoe" had other commitments for the Derby and chose to ride the California horse Hill Rise. The Taylor people went with Bill Hartack.

On Saturday, May 2nd, 1964, when the field of twelve colts went to the post for the 90th annual running of the Kentucky Derby at Churchill Downs, Hill Rise was the favorite at 7 to 5. Northern Dancer was second choice at the rather attractive price of 7 to 2.

A few frenzied minutes later, Jim Coleman was back at his typewriter again pounding out the words:

"The hero of this place is the Fastest Canadian on Four Feet. Northern Dancer, our pugnacious little horse with the musculature of a perfectly-conditioned heavyweight, ran a hole in the wind as he shattered the Kentucky Derby record for a mile and one-quarter."

Back home in Canada, the millions who had watched the Derby on television were all but dancing in the streets. Without question, it was the most important victory in the history of Canadian horse racing.

Two weeks later, Northern Dancer won the Preakness, but came third in the Belmont Stakes, losing a bid for the Triple Crown. Still, he was voted North America's three-year-old champion for 1964 by turf writers.

Taylor's bantam colt was hailed as a national hero when he came home to Toronto for the last race of his career, the Queen's Plate, on June 20th, 1964. A crowd of 32,000 applauded hysterically as Bill Hartack rode the Dancer to an easy victory over seven courageous but outclassed rivals.

A few weeks after his win in Toronto, while the colt was training at Belmont Park, he bowed a tendon in his left foreleg. To the lamentations of the entire Canadian nation, it was necessary to retire him to the breeding farm. But, it was on the farm that he was to achieve even greater glory — he became the most successful stallion in North America.

For more than two decades after his victories on the track, Canadians thrilled as Northern Dancer's progeny established themselves as the best thoroughbreds in Europe and North America.

Coleman writes: "He was, unquestionably, the most explosive and potent hunk of horseflesh ever to be born on Canadian soil. We shall be boundlessly fortunate and twice-blessed if we ever see his like again."

39

Jim Marshall
This way Jim!

Every defensive end in football will tell you it's a dream of his to score a touchdown, but Jim Marshall would rather forget the one he scored on October 26th, 1964 while playing for the Minnesota Vikings of the NFL.

It was at San Francisco's Kezar Stadium. While playing against the

·49ers, Marshall watched as quarterback George Mira attempted a short lateral pass. The receiver caught the ball but coughed it up moments later. Marshall recovered and, after eluding a few tackles, found his way into the open and began a mad dash for the goal line with only a handful of teammates in pursuit.

Yes ... teammates!

Desperately, the Vikings' players yelled at Marshall, but he only heard the roar of the crowd as he sprinted 66 yards into the end zone ... his own end zone!

Instead of six points for the Vikings, it was the 49ers who were awarded two points for a safety.

Humiliated, Jim Marshall could only say afterwards — "I saw my teammates running down the sidelines yelling at me. I thought they were cheering for me!"

Fortunately for Marshall, the Vikings won the game 27-22 and his teammates would only tease him over the miscue.

40

Pele
The King of Soccer

In 1951, a retired soccer player in Brazil by the name of Waldemar de Brito happened by a construction site where some workmen were playing a little soccer after their shift. Darting like a hummingbird through and around men twice his size and age was a skinny, undernourished eleven-year-old boy. De Brito was astonished by what he saw. This boy was able to keep control of the ball almost magically. The old player recognized a phenomenon when he saw one, even in such diminutive form.

He spent the next four years working with the young lad, whose name was Edson Arantes do Nascimento.

After polishing the young Edson's natural gifts and co-ordination those four years, De Brito bought him his first pair of long trousers and got the boy's parents' permission to take him to Santos, Brazil's great coffee port. There he presented the awed 15-year-old youngster to the directors of the Santos Football Club with the grandoise introduction; "This boy will be the greatest soccer player in the world."

Thrown into practice with veteran pros, Edson quickly demonstrated that his discoverer was no mean prophet. He had always relied on his wit and speed to beat older, bigger players, and he continued to do just that. Almost immediately the Santos team signed him up for 6,000 cruzeiros (about $50.00) a month. In 1956, in his first professional game, Santos won, 7-1. Edson scored four of the seven goals.

Within a year, the ex-shoeshine boy, now sixteen, and the youngest player ever to star as a pro, had become a legend throughout his homeland. Brazil's soccer crowds decided they had never seen a player quite like him. Loping or sprinting, he could drag the ball from one foot to the other as if it were a yo-yo on the end of an invisible string. When trapped by the defence, he had an uncanny ability to flick a pass into an open spot for a teammate to pick up. He could head the ball with bullseye precision, kick straight as an arrow with either foot or use a "banana shot" to make the ball curve.

More important, sportswriters noted that the rising star was a master tactician. Cool, unruffled even when being rushed, he had the ability to plot elaborate offensive plays on the spur of the moment. Intuitively, at any given instant, he seemed to know the position of all other players on the field, and he sensed just what each man was going to do next. This was Edson's greatest gift — a talent for sparking any eleven man team into a formidable tactical machine.

Meanwhile — nobody knows how or why — Edson had acquired the name Pele. Oddly enough, it means absolutely nothing. It can be best described to a non-Brazilian as a nonsense term of affection.

Pele burst into international prominence during the World Cup competition in Stockholm in 1958. Then only 17 and limping from a knee injury, he broke a scoreless game against Wales with a dazzling play that

75

soccer fans still talk about. With his back towards the Welsh goal, Pele, with his right foot, suddenly kicked the ball into a gentle arc back over his own ducking head. Then, as it bounced off a surprised Welsh player, he spun around and, with his left foot sent the ball sizzling into the Welsh net for the winning goal. All without the ball ever having touched the ground!

The newcomer was equally brilliant in the final against Sweden, scoring two spectacular goals in a 5-2 win that claimed the World Cup for Brazil.

After that World Cup debut and continued marvellous play in international matches (he also led Brazil to World Cups in 1962 and 1970), journalists began to exhaust their superlatives in writing about the incomparable Pele. In Italy, he was "Il Re", "The King"; in France, "La Tulipe Noir", "The Black Tulip"; in Chile, he was "El Peligro", "The Peril." To his fellow Brazilians, he was not only "The King" but also "Perola Negra", "The Black Pearl." During his reign, Pele's beaming face was a weekly fixture on the Brazilian sports pages, and his hoarse-voiced radio talk to the nation after a match was followed more avidly than a presidential address.

Between 1960 and 1964, Pele effectively nailed down the status that old de Brito had predicted so boldly when introducing him. In the 1962 World Cup championship against Portugal's tough Benfica team in Lisbon, Pele put on another incredibly dominant display, scoring three goals and creating two other easy tap-ins for his teammates in a 5-2 Santos victory.

"It was the greatest single performance by a player for years," wrote Brian Glanville in the *London Sunday Times*.

Because of his stellar play, Pele was subjected to more attention and more punishment than is normal for any soccer player. For years opponents tried to stop him by holding, tripping or kicking. He was badly hurt many times and often had to take novocaine injections in order to continue playing. During a series in Mexico, he once starred while playing with one arm in a sling!

After playing with Santos from 1956 to 1974, Pele accepted an offer that interested him for financial reasons and because of his love for his game. He went to the United States to play for the New York Cosmos of the North American Soccer League. His arrival gave the sport a much-needed dose of credibility and a major gate attraction. He played for the Cosmos for three years for a huge salary — some said as much as $7 million. But the game thrived and during his tenure the Cosmos won the NASL championship, beating Seattle 2-1 on August 28, 1977 in Pele's last game in the league.

He scored 1281 goals over his career, including 65 in his three years in North America, and retired a rich man. Pele's position as reigning monarch of his game was crystalized when, in 1962, Prince Philip, the Duke of Edinburgh paid an official visit to Brazil and expressed a desire to see Pele play and to compliment him personally either before or after the game. For days, Brazilian diplomats were faced with a dilemma: "Should the Prince go down to the field to greet Pele or should Pele step up to the dais to be complimented by the Prince?"

The Prince solved the problem himself. Before the game he went down to the field in Sao Paulo Stadium to shake hands with Pele. Commenting on this, a Brazilian journalist wrote: "In the kingdom of soccer, to whose territory all the states of the world belong, the only king is Pele. Above his majesty only the spiritual power of heaven can rule."

41

Brant Alyea
Of Sandlots and Sandinistas

The Toronto Blue Jays have, in their farm system, a young prospect whose father was a major-leaguer. That's not so special; there are numerous "chips off the old block" out there, trying to make it in the game their dads played. But this story is different. This "chip off the old block" was a love-child, born into a war zone his father had to flee.

Brant Alyea spent six seasons as a powerhitting yet part-time outfielder with four different major league teams. He is now forty-eight years old and works as floorman in a casino in Atlantic City, New Jersey, near his home town of Passaic.

Today, major leaguers can keep their baseball skills sharp by playing through the winter in professional leagues in some of the Latin American baseball hotbeds like Venezuela, the Dominican Republic, Puerto Rico and Mexico. Once upon a time, Nicaragua was among the countries that welcomed pro baseball players on their way up to or down from the big leagues.

In 1966 there was an incredible championship game in Nicaragua between Cinco Estrellas and La Boer. As the game ended, the revolution began. The American players had to run from gunfire and from the country. Brant Alyea was one of the players in that ill-fated game. As it turned out, he would leave more than the echoes of gunfire behind in Nicaragua.

"On the night the shooting started, I thought I'd be smart, so I put my luggage at the Grand Hotel, only to discover the next day that tanks had surrounded the place and my luggage had been confiscated. I left anyway with the rest of the guys, bricks hitting our taxi windows, the whole frightening scene. Since I had no luggage, I was the first person to pass through customs when we reached the U.S. The reporters zeroed in on me and started asking questions. I knew better than to say anything political. I could only say 'I'm a ballplayer. There's a lot of turmoil down there and I don't know what's happening.'

"What I didn't tell them was that I had left a baby son down there. I didn't want anything to happen to him or his mother.

"I had played in Nicaragua one year earlier, you see, in 1965, the same year I was a rookie with the Washington Senators. While there, I dated a Nicaraguan girl, Melania Medina, a nurse in a hospital. We saw a lot of each other but we left it at that. When winter ball was finished, I went back to the States. When I returned again in 1966, one of the Nicaraguan players on the team met me at the plane and said, 'Come with me, I want to show you something.' And he took me to the Medina home where I found Melania holding a baby. She said it was mine and I had no reason to doubt her. The family was very apprehensive, not because we were unmarried, but because they wanted the baby to have my name. So I signed the papers and there was a big fiesta, everyone hugging each other. They were all happy now because the baby had my name and there would be no shame. It was fine and Melania brought the baby to games all season.

"Then all hell broke loose. Before I left the country I left Melania $1,000 and told her I'd be back. But I couldn't get back. I kept track of them for a while through the child's godfather, a Cuban ballplayer named Pancho Herrera. He sent me a report once, when the boy was ten, that he had gotten big and was playing baseball in the streets. Melania, meanwhile, married a man who lives in Venezuela and she is allowed to come and go between her native country and Venezuela. Only men cannot leave Nicaragua.

"As time passed, I lost track of the boy, but never the awareness that he was there. When I'd see the fighting in the streets of Nicaragua on television I'd say to friends, 'It feels strange to know I have a son down there, perhaps one of those kids holding a gun.'

"Then, around 1985, we were standing around in the casino in Atlantic City talking baseball and one of the bosses had this magazine that listed seventy major leaguers who had sons playing professional ball. And there it was: Brant Alyea Jr. was hitting .333 for Medicine Hat in a rookie league in Canada.

"It was my kid and he was a pro ball player and I didn't even know it! So I rushed to the phone and contacted him through the Blue Jays. Apparently he had wanted to reach me but didn't speak any English. We eventually hooked up the following spring at the Blue Jays spring training site near Clearwater and, yeah, there were some tears. But, I want to tell you, this kid is going to be a player. It turns out that at age seventeen he was 6'4", 170 and the best player in Nicaragua. That's why he didn't have to go into the army. He just played ball.

"How he got out of the country is the damndest thing. First he went to Canada to play for Nicaragua in a 10-day tournament against Cuba,

Canada and the U.S. He was the tournament MVP and that's where the Blue Jays spotted him. They sent their ace Latin American scout to Nicaragua. He dressed in a Sandinista uniform to gain entry into the stadium to see Brant play. There was no way they wanted this kid to leave the country to play ball in America.

"So the Jays offer him a contract and he signs for $6,000 bonus and gives the money to his mother. Now the Blue Jays have to figure out how to get him out. He lives with his aunt in Nicaragua, so they send her $2,000 to use as bribe money. They went to the airport where they said Brant was flying to Venezuela to visit his mother. The soldiers weren't going to let him go at first, but the $2,000 changed their minds.

"It turns out that when he was playing ball as a kid down there he took great pride in being my son. He was motivated because a lot of people remember me. I had led the league in home runs both years I was there and he had seen old pictures of me.

"So he's a hot prospect, learning the game in the Blue Jays farm system, playing winter ball in Venezuela, and staying with me when he's between seasons. I think it's great. He still calls his friends in Nicaragua but he knows he can't go back, just like I couldn't twenty years ago."

42

Ken Stabler
It's Alabam' or Uncle Sam!

"Play hard, live fast and throw deep!"

That was the motto of one of the most famous and effective quarterbacks ever to play football. Ken Stabler played 15 seasons in the NFL, passed for almost 28,000 yards, played in three Pro Bowls (NFL all-star games), and led the Oakland Raiders to victory in Super Bowl XI in January of 1977.

The lanky left-hander, known as "Snake," was a master of picking apart defences not with overpowering velocity on his passes, but with pinpoint accuracy. The statistic by which quarterbacks like to be measured is "completion percentage." Stabler's completion percentage over his 15 year career with three NFL teams was a remarkable 59.85.

But Stabler, especially during his years with the Oakland Raiders, was known as much for his off-the-field carousing as he was for his skills. Teammates and opponents marvelled at his ability to drink and chase women all night, and then show up Sunday afternoon and throw four touchdown passes and lead the Raiders to a win.

"Yeah, we all indulged quite a bit," Stabler once told me during a 1986 interview about his new book — a no-holds-barred biography.

"With some of the crazies on that team, I can remember some genuine 100-proof huddles out there some Sundays."

Stabler was an old hand at combining the partying and football, though, having perfected the art while he was a college star at Alabama.

As a junior, Stabler won the MVP award, leading the Crimson Tide to a 34-7 win over Nebraska in the 1967 Sugar Bowl. But he tore a cartilage in his knee in spring practice that year. Arthroscopic surgery hadn't been invented yet, so Stabler was told to rest through the spring. The team doctors at Alabama felt he'd be healthy for the season in the fall, his senior season.

As it turned out, Stabler took his coach, Paul "Bear" Bryant too literally when the coach told him "Don't do anything Kenny; just let that knee heal."

Bored with watching from the sidelines as his teammates worked out, Stabler, ever the skirt-chaser and adventurer, took to driving from the university campus in Tuscaloosa down to Mobile Bay on Alabama's Gulf Coast to see a girl. The drive was four hours and Stabler was making the trip down and back three or four nights a week. He'd leave campus at nine in the evening, right after study hall ended, and would try to make it back for an eight o'clock morning class the next day. Soon he began skipping study hall, then skipping the early morning class. He started failing, even with the light course load given football players. He had picked up dozens of speeding tickets on the Alabama highways, and even stopped showing up on the sidelines at football practice.

Naturally, word of his transgressions reached the athletic department. So he kind of expected to hear from Coach Bryant. But he didn't expect to hear about it the way he did. It was a simple telegram. Stabler received it when he was home visiting his parents one weekend. "YOU HAVE BEEN INDEFINITELY SUSPENDED," it read. "COACH PAUL W. BRYANT." He didn't waste any words.

Stabler wondered if the coach was serious. He remembered how Bryant had suspended another star quarterback at Alabama, Joe Namath, for some hell-raising before the 1963 season. But would he suspend Stabler, after his quarterback had led the team to an 11-0 record and a Sugar Bowl win and been named MVP?

A few hours later, Stabler got another telegram, this one from Joe Namath. His read: "HE MEANS IT!"

Soon, Stabler received official notice that his grade-point average had fallen below the minimum required level for intercollegiate athletic eligibility. He could no longer play football.

"The Snake" was miffed, and decided to say, "To hell with all of you." He began several weeks of revelry on the Gulf Coast, an area he liked to call, "The Redneck Riviera." He didn't care about anything but having a good time. Twice he ran into an assistant coach from the Alabama football team, who was down in the Mobile area doing some recruiting. Both times, the coach pleaded with Stabler to come back to campus, get serious about school and make his peace with Bear Bryant. Stabler wasn't interested.

Ultimately, it was his father who tricked him into going back.

Slim Stabler, a garage mechanic in Ken's hometown of Foley, had a lawyer friend write a letter from the United States Army Draft Board, saying if Ken did not return to college by the fall, he would be subject to induction.

Stabler took that letter to be genuine. The Vietnam War was hot in the spring of 1967, and he had no interest in getting shot. In June he went back to school, enrolled in summer session, regained his eligibility, and, after some confrontational moments with Bear Bryant, came out for the team again. As punishment, Bryant made Stabler start the training camp on the sixth-string team, and did not start him in the opening game.

He did eventually get his starting job back though, and had a good season in his senior year, although Alabama lost the Cotton Bowl 20-16 that year to Texas A & M.

In the spring of 1968, Stabler, who had been a good pitcher before quitting baseball to concentrate fully on football, was chosen by baseball's Houston Astros in the second round of the free agent draft. But he opted for football's Oakland Raiders when they picked him, also in the second round.

After a couple of trying seasons early on, plagued by knee trouble and homesickness, Stabler matured into one of the craftiest and most efficient quarterbacks the game has ever seen.

43

Bob Beamon
Jumping for Joy

World records aren't exactly a dime a dozen, but they do get broken with regularity in Olympic Games if for no other reason than that the quadrennial contests provide the athletes with their greatest competition. The athletes who gathered at Mexico City in 1968 knew that, but they also knew that the 1½-mile-high altitude was going to play havoc with some events. In track and field, the jumpers and short-distance runners were supposed to benefit the most, for the higher one goes above sea level, the thinner the air is. That in turn makes for less resistance.

Bob Beamon, a stork-like American long jumper, had all the facts on file as he prepared for the Olympic finals. He had easily made the U.S. team with a wind-aided jump of 27 feet 6½ inches − the longest ever but not a record because of the wind factor.

Though he was the youngest jumper in the field at age 22, and despite the fact that he would be matched against three of the greatest jumpers of all time, he was the favorite to win in Mexico City. Most experts felt that he, or whoever won, would have to jump 28 feet. Competition and altitude would force the athletes to break the 28-foot barrier for the first time.

The 1968 long-jump field was clearly the greatest ever. Along with Beamon there was Ralph Boston, the 1960 gold medalist and 1964 runner-up; Igor Ter-Ovanesyan, an Olympic veteran who shared the world record of 27 feet 4¾ inches with Boston; and Lynn Davies, the man who upset Boston at Tokyo in 1964. Boston was an American, Ter-Ovanesyan a Russian, and Davies a Britisher.

Despite the formidable field, Beamon remained the favorite. Having high-jumped 6 feet 5 inches, and being a 9.5-second sprinter, he had all the tools to lift his lanky frame over 28 feet. Competitively, he brought a string of 22 straight victories with him to Mexico City.

Beamon may have been feeling the pressures as competition got underway. He nearly fouled out in the qualifying round as he kept missing his steps. One of those fouled jumps was for 27 feet 6 inches, further than the world record, and a foot further than the existing Olympic record. But with the foul, it was merely a piece of trivia for the track and field buffs.

Altogether, Beamon fouled twice and scratched twice. He had one last jump in which to qualify for the finals. So he shortened his stride to choppy steps and landed safely at 26 feet 10½ inches. That advanced him to the finals.

Beamon decided that his way of avoiding the pressure in the finals would be to make his best effort on his initial jump — and let the others resolve the psychological problem if he was successful. The other three, meanwhile, were already toying with Beamon's unlimited potential in their minds. "I'm always nervous when Beamon goes down the runway," said Boston, "because you know that some day he's going to put all that great talent together in one big jump."

There were 17 jumpers in the finals on a mid-October day, and three of them were jumping before Beamon. With the temperature cooling, making the artificial runway harder and confusing to figure out, Beamon watched all three foul. Beamon took that into consideration as he roared down the track for his first leap. He hit the board perfectly without breaking stride, and lifted himself like a bird. A slight but legal 2-meters-per-second breeze helped carry him through the air. When he landed, he jumped for joy, knowing he had done well.

An official notified him that his leap was 8.90 meters. Bob knew that 8.60 meters equalled 28 feet 2¾ inches, which was his goal, so he was even more excited. Someone quickly converted the 8.90 for him; it equalled an astounding 29 feet 2½ inches — 16 inches over the world record!

Beamon went into a daze and kissed the earth he had leaped over. "Tell me I'm not dreaming," he asked of anyone who approached him. The track buffs figured that a 29-foot 2½-inch jump was comparable to a 3:43.3 mile or a 7-foot 10½-inch high jump, two statistics that had not even come close to being approached.

Beamon's initial jump was enough for victory. The other jumpers wilted under the strain of thinking about it. Davies could jump only 21 feet 1¾ inches on his next try. Boston just shook his head in awe.

Cordner Nelson, editor of *Track & Field News* and an observer of many track feats while covering six Olympics, wrote later that Beamon had given "probably the greatest single performance in the history of the sport."

44

NBC-TV
The Heidi Game

Gaffs and glitches in the slick world of network television are not that common. When they do occur, they are glaring and are noticed and complained about by a lot of viewers. Rarely has there been one as glaring and as resounding as the now-famous "Heidi Game" on NBC. As it turned out, it was no glitch, it was a programming decision that went down in infamy.

On November 17, 1968, the New York Jets and the Oakland Raiders clashed in Oakland in what was a battle of the American Football League powerhouses. A Jets victory would assure them of at least a tie for their first Eastern Division championship. The Raiders needed a win to stay in contention in the Western Division.

Because of the importance of the game, it was shown live across the entire NBC network, beginning at 4:30 p.m. New York time.

As anticipated, the game was closely fought and at half time the Raiders led 14-12. Most fans didn't notice that the game was taking longer than normal because of penalties, injuries and first-down measurements.

When the game resumed, the action began to pick up considerably. The teams traded touchdowns in the third quarter and Oakland led 22-19 as they entered the final fifteen minutes. After an Oakland fumble, the Jets scored ten unanswered points on a Joe Namath to Don Maynard touchdown pass and Jim Turner's third field goal of the game. With nine minutes remaining, the Jets held a 29-22 lead.

Sensing the importance of the game, Oakland quarterback Daryle

Lamonica marched his team downfield and hit Fred Biletnikoff with a 22-yard touchdown pass. That tied the score 29-29 with four minutes left. Not to be outdone, Namath led the Jets back downfield and into field goal range. Turner's fourth field goal of the game gave the Jets the 32-29 lead with only 65 seconds to go.

But, the game was not over. New York fans cringed as a 20-yard pass completion and a 15-yard penalty gave the Raiders the ball on the Jets 43-yard line with plenty of time left.

At this point, the nail-biting action was interrupted by a commercial. A station break followed the commercial. Then, to everyone's surprise, the NBC peacock appeared on the screen and viewers were informed that the following program would be in living colour.

What appeared next was "The Story of Heidi" — a children's special! Football fans went berserk! Where was the game?

The NBC switchboard was swamped with phone calls. The network finally decided to return to the game but it was too late — the game was over and viewers had missed the conclusion.

Unknown to television viewers, debate had occurred between NBC executives when it became obvious that the football telecast would run late. It was argued that millions of children would be tuning in to see "The Story of Heidi" at 7 p.m. To finish carrying the football game and start "Heidi" late would mean some parts of the children's program would have to be cut. After the Jets scored with 65 seconds left, the decision was made that "Heidi" would begin promptly at 7 o'clock. The NBC execs reasoned that the game was pretty much over as Oakland would not have time to score again.

As it happened, the Raiders not only had time to score once, but twice!

As soon as "Heidi" went on the air, Daryle Lamonica threw a 43-yard touchdown pass to put Oakland up 36-32. The Jets then fumbled the ensuing kickoff and Oakland recovered for a touchdown and the final score was 43-32 for the Raiders.

As far as New York fans knew though, the Jets had escaped with a 32-29 victory — with some help from a little girl named "Heidi."

45

The 1969 CFL Playoffs
A November to Remember

The 1969 Canadian Football League season will be remembered for several things; early on, Calgary argued about shoes, Toronto made much ado about walking-around money, and in the end, Ottawa's Russ Jackson "walked on water."

During June training camps, the Calgary Stampeders demanded that team management start picking up the tab for their football shoes. It was a public issue for a while, but, eventually, the matter was settled. Stamps General Manager, Rogers Lehew, declined to say who had won the battle of the cleats, but it was duly noticed that the boys from Canada's oil capital were well shod during that season.

In Toronto, the rhubarb was about expense money for players during the seven-week training camp. They wanted $60 a week for everybody, plus $40 a week retroactive to the start of training for the 32 players who made the squad. There were grumblings from one side about "a walkout," and from the other side about "suspensions." It was finally settled amicably enough, and the season got under way.

The Argonauts, under coach Leo Cahill, played well all season, showing they belonged with the top clubs in the league. That is until the playoffs.

They had battled the defending Grey Cup champion Ottawa Rough Riders down to the wire in three league meetings and had displayed lots of muscle in games East and West. They were cocky and confident as they approached the playoffs. They had lost 25-23, 34-27 and 20-9 to Ottawa in games that could have gone either way.

Finally, they broke through in the first game of a two-game, total-point Eastern Conference final, beating the Riders 22-14. Every long suffering Argo fan climbed aboard the bandwagon.

This was the "next year" that fans had been talking about since 1952 when the Toronto club had last made the Cup final. They couldn't see how their team could lose now. Even Cahill got into the act, saying, "It will take an act of God to beat us." He followed that up with the pronouncement that the Argonauts were "physically better than any team in Canada."

The Ottawa Rough Riders weren't impressed with the Argo talk — or muscle.

On Saturday, November 22, they clobbered the Argos 32-3 and ended up with a 45-25 advantage in the total point playoff.

Ottawa fans took great delight in shoving Cahill's biblical bravado back down his throat. They suggested there had been an "act of God" in the form of Russ Jackson, the great Ottawa quarterback, whom they suggested did not ride that day to Lansdowne Park, but merely strode across the Rideau Canal on the ice floes. Others playfully clucked that Cahill could have dressed the Twelve Apostles in Argo uniforms that day and Jackson and company would have whipped them as easily.

The Riders did go on to win the Grey Cup the next week at the Autostade in Montreal. It was Russ Jackson's farewell to football after 12 seasons, during which he quarterbacked the Ottawa club to three Cup titles. And in this, his final year, Jackson won every personal award and honor worth winning.

In the Grey Cup Game, the crafty 32-year-old saw plenty of close-ups of the pass rushers from Regina, but he squirmed, ducked, back-pedalled, and passed his way to a 29-11 Ottawa win over Saskatchewan. He threw four touchdown passes — a Cup record — including a pair to his long-time backfield mate, Ron Stewart, another 12-year man who played one of the finest games of his brilliant career. It had been back in 1960 that "Stewie", a five-foot-seven, 175 pound halfback out of Queen's University, had carried the ball 15 times, scored four touchdowns and racked up 287 yards, a Canadian single-game record.

Here, nine years later, he was fabulous again in the clutch, bursting for touchdowns of 80 and 32 yards.

Jackson, though, was named player of the game, to go with his league MVP award and selection to conference and league all-star teams.

But there were more honours still to come for Russ Jackson that year. On December 19, he was one of 22 Canadians to receive the medal of service of the Order of Canada. Selections are made for "merit, especially service to Canada at large." At the end of the year, Jackson was named Canadian Press Athlete of the Year, and later, in another CP poll was named Most Newsworthy Canadian outside public affairs.

Not bad for a kid from Hamilton, who starred for McMaster University and then jumped into the CFL in 1957. And fitting that he should reach such heights at his chosen vocation, because Jackson chose professional football instead of a Rhodes Scholarship when he graduated.

Russ Jackson is now a high school principal in the Toronto area.

The Argos finally won the Grey Cup again in 1983.

46

Brian Spencer
Spinning Out of Control

For all its glamour, professional sports is a world littered with broken dreams and broken lives, but perhaps none is a more tragic and heart-wrenching story than that of Brian "Spinner" Spencer.

An affable, rough-around-the-edges kid from the wilds of the northern British Columbia interior, he played hockey from 1970 to 1979 for the Toronto Maple Leafs, the New York Islanders, the Buffalo Sabres and finally, the Pittsburgh Penguins.

In his 10 years in the NHL, he scored only 80 goals, but did make it once to the Stanley Cup playoffs with Buffalo and managed four assists in the series, which the Sabres eventually lost to Philadelphia. Nevertheless, "The Spin," as he was nicknamed for his unorthodox skating style, was always respected by opposing players and by fans for his fearlessness and his gritty hustle. He was extremely popular in his day.

But, tragedy stalked Spencer virtually from the start of his NHL career. Just before Christmas 1970, he was called up from the Leafs' farm team at Tulsa. He arrived just in time to help the Leafs beat Montreal 4-0 on a Wednesday night. Thursday, his wife gave birth to a baby girl. He telephoned home to Fort St. James to tell his family and to tell them he was playing in Saturday night's game against Chicago, which was to be telecast live from coast to coast on the CBC, and he was to be interviewed by Ward Cornell during the intermission.

Brian Spencer's father Roy, a wiry Scottish immigrant, had been an irascible drillmaster during his son's early hockey development. He drove the lad mercilessly during the freezing winters on the family's outdoor rink, berating him, and once even going so far as to throw surprise body checks at him during skating drills to "toughen him up." Still, no one was prouder when Brian made it to the Maple Leafs, and Roy had never seen his son play pro hockey, never seen him play on television. He was thrilled to hear Brian would be on TV Saturday night.

On the morning of the game, Roy Spencer finished his chores early at the family farm in Fort St. James so he could be ready for *Hockey Night in Canada,* which started at 5 o'clock in the afternoon in B.C. The father prepared himself for the game as he imagined his son would be doing in Toronto. He ate a "game-day" steak, as he heard hockey players did, then took a light nap, thinking about the game, as the big-leaguers are told to do. The game coming up that night was the talk of the town in Fort St. James and Roy Spencer basked in the reflected glory.

When he awoke, just before game time, Roy heard the news that the CBC television station in his area, in nearby Prince George, wouldn't be carrying the Toronto-Chicago game, but would pick up the Vancouver Canucks-California Golden Seals game instead. Roy phoned CKPG-TV in Prince George and was told it was a network decision and wouldn't be changed. That was when he snapped.

He jumped in his car with a .303 rifle and twelve rounds of ammunition, a 9-mm Belgian automatic pistol and three hunting knives. He drove to Prince George, walked into the local TV station and held eight staff members at gunpoint, ranting about the "CBC's coverage." At 7:40 p.m. local time, 10:40 p.m. Toronto time, someone pulled a switch and CKPG went off the air. Roy Spencer backed out the front door, still holding a pistol on the station employees, saying he didn't want to kill anyone. He turned to find the RCMP waiting for him. For whatever reason, when they ordered him to "hold it!", Roy whirled and fired. Two Mounties were hit, they returned fire and Roy Spencer was killed. As he died in a snowbank in Prince George, his son Brian was being interviewed by Ward Cornell on *Hockey Night in Canada*. He had played well and the Leafs had won 2-1.

Brian Spencer was informed in the middle of the night in Toronto of the events leading to his father's death. Strangely, he carried on. The Leafs played in Buffalo the next night and won 4-0; Spencer notched two assists, won a fight and was named one of the three stars of the game by Foster Hewitt.

He flew to Fort St. James for the funeral the following Thursday, at which he read from a crumpled telegram his father had sent to him before the Chicago game that was to have been televised. The telegram read: "Give 'em hell son. We are mighty proud."

That tragedy befell Brian Spencer when he was 21. Tragedy was to be a running-mate of his ten years later as well.

After his hockey career ended, Spencer drifted eventually to Florida and worked at odd jobs in the seedy backwater area in and around West Palm Beach. Falling in with the wrong types here and there, he was in and out of trouble with the police for drunk driving, but things got serious when, in January 1987, detectives arrested Spencer and charged him with a murder committed five years earlier. When he was arrested, he was carrying most of his life's possessions in a battered attaché case that had been presented to him fifteen years earlier when he left the Maple Leafs to go to play for the New York Islanders. There was still an "Islanders" decal on the attaché case, just below the handle.

Inside the case were old hockey clippings, snapshots, press kits, team programs, bubblegum hockey cards. There was a wire-service photo of his first NHL goal, a flattering article from a 1971 Maple Leaf Gardens program, a glossy formal portrait of him and his first wife, Linda, looking down at their infant daughter, old, curled head-and-shoulders photos of former Leaf teammates: Armstrong, Pulford, Keon, Ullman, Henderson, Ellis. And odd things — a placemat from the Sweet William restaurant in Cleveland, on the back of which is a detailed pencil sketch of a monstrous van-truck, and a well-preserved red portfolio with a swastika on the front above the gold-embossed letters that read: "Adolf Hitler. Confidential. My political testament."

After some time in jail, there was a long and well-publicized trial that fall where the innocence or guilt of Brian Spencer was debated and, finally, he was acquitted. During his trial, hundreds of letters of support had flowed in from across Canada and the U.S., and several former hockey teammates came to Florida to stand by their old friend. Upon his acquittal, Spencer was ready to start afresh. He had a job, a new woman in his life and was looking forward to putting the agony of the trial behind him. He managed to ... for eight months.

Then tragedy stalked Brian Spencer once again and caught up with him in June of 1988.

He and a friend were sitting in a truck on a dark street in West Palm Beach, about to go into a 7-Eleven store for cigarettes when a man walked up to the driver's window and pointed a gun in, demanding money. Spencer's friend coughed up the three dollars in his pocket. When the gunman turned to Spencer, the old defiance showed — borne out of a rugged boyhood in a tough town, out of a thousand hockey battles — he shrugged, said he had no money and looked away. Without hesitation, the gunman reached across the driver and shot Spencer in the chest.

Brian Spencer died within minutes.

47

Larry Robinson
Battling the Bottles....

The road to a professional hockey career is one strewn with obstacles, not the least of which is coping with the rigors and demands of junior hockey.

Canadian junior hockey is a rough, tough, grind that makes teenagers leave home right around the time they are old enough to drive, often ends any legitimate chance at academic pursuits, and thrusts them into a milieu where they must battle every day to survive, and to be noticed by the pros.

In the 1970-71 hockey season, in his one and only year of 'major junior A,' Larry Robinson, later to become a splendid defenceman with the Montreal Canadiens, paid his dues in other places besides on the blueline for the Kitchener Rangers.

When Robinson was 19, he became a father. After learning that his girlfriend, Jeannette, had become pregnant, Robinson quickly married her — his hometown sweetheart from Marveleville, Ontario, outside Ottawa. That was in June of 1970. When most junior-aged hockey players head off to play in a strange city for the winter, they carry with them their hockey gear and their dreams of the NHL. When Larry Robinson headed off for the Kitchener Rangers that fall, he carried with him a wife and a newborn baby. His thoughts were as much about how to make ends meet as they were of the NHL.

How he made ends meet was to hold down an extra job in addition to playing hockey for the Rangers.

Robinson was earning $60 per week from the hockey club. The apartment where he, Jeannette and their son Jeffery lived, cost $150 per month. For the extra cash, the rangy defenceman lugged pop crates at the Kitchener Beverages plant during the day, while at night he battled the likes of Denis Potvin, Steve Shutt, Marcel Dionne and other future NHL stars when they rolled into Kitchener with their respective junior teams.

Junior hockey road trips are almost exclusively bus trips — sometimes long bus trips. Kitchener to Ottawa is a good 5 to 6 hours. Sometimes Robinson would arrive back in Kitchener in the middle of the night from a road game, and have to be in to sling pop crates at 8 a.m. He'd be there all day, then off to a practice or a game after his day at work. His wife was rarely able to go to the games, as that would mean hiring a babysitter, something the penny-conscious Robinsons could ill afford. They also found difficulty socializing with other players and their girlfriends. Larry was the only one on the team who was married, and he had a baby to look out for. Something as simple as going out for a beer with teammates after a Saturday night game didn't happen often. Larry Robinson and his young wife say they sometimes felt deprived of their late teen years.

The following spring, after a strong junior season in Kitchener, Robinson was drafted in the first round by the Montreal Canadiens. He has gone on to star for that team for 17 seasons, being an integral part of six Stanley Cup winning teams, many times an all-star, and a member of Canada Cup winning teams in 1976 and 1984. He is also still happily married to Jeannette, and as well as Jeffery, they have a daughter, Rachelle.

In the summer of 1989, after 17 years with the Montreal Canadiens, Larry Robinson moved to the west coast to accept a free agent contract with the Los Angeles Kings, to finish his career alongside Wayne Gretzky. Son Jeffery is considered a solid NHL prospect himself — as a goaltender.

48

Istvan Gaal
Kicked

Istvan Gaal was such a disappointment to his team in the National Soccer League that, in 1971, he was traded to a rival team...for a soccer ball!

"I think it was a very fair trade," said John Fischer, president of the Kitchener Concordia Kickers of the Canadian semi professional league. "Both teams got what they wanted."

Gaal was a player whose skills apparently couldn't be measured by money. There was no cash involved in the swap with the Toronto Hungarians. It was a straight player-for-ball deal.

"We didn't give him away for nothing," Fischer insisted. "We got a regulation National Soccer League ball in return for him. They go for $27.50."

Long before the trade, Gaal, a 21-year-old Hungarian defector who claimed he had scored thirty-one goals in forty-four games back in his native country, had been considered a prize catch. In fact, the Kickers went to extraordinary means to sign him — they kidnapped him. Gaal had agreed to terms with Toronto, but while he was standing on a street corner in Toronto with a team representative, a black car screeched to a halt in front of them. Two men hustled Gaal off to Kitchener, where he was persuaded to join the Kickers.

Unfortunately, he turned out to be a big letdown, said Fischer. "He had a few moves, but he looked bad. At first we thought he was holding back. He had just come to a new country and couldn't speak the language. We thought he'd be okay once he adjusted. But he never improved."

Gaal was so bad he couldn't even make it as a sub on the Kickers, who were thirteenth in a fourteen-team league. So a deal was struck with Toronto.

Recalled Fischer, "The Toronto team said to me, 'Why don't you just release the guy to us?' I said, 'Hell no, I'm not going to give him away for nothing. You send me that soccer ball.' They said they would and they did."

"The trade wasn't all that unique," added Fischer. "I went through some records and found a hockey player who had once been traded for a pair of nets."

49

No Shows
Timing is Everything

It was 4:15 in the afternoon. Eddie Hart and Rey Robinson, two American sprinters, were sitting in their rooms in the Olympic Village in Munich, watching the 1972 Olympics on television. They were relaxing before their quarter-final heat in the 100-metre sprint, scheduled for 6:15 that evening. Or so they thought.

Suddenly, they realized what they were watching on television — it was the preliminaries for THEIR RACE!

They dashed into a car and tried to make it to the stadium, but by the time they got there, their race was over.

How could they have been wrong about the start time?

Checking the timetables, it was discovered the time was properly posted as starting at "1615h." The coach failed to realize the schedulers used the 24-hour clock.

He told his runners their race was at 6:15.

(Sixteen years later, at the 1988 Summer Games in Seoul, failure to read the events timetable correctly again cost an American athlete his chance to compete after years of training and preparation.

Anthony Hembrick, a boxer, missed his bout at the Chamsil Students Gymnasium because the coaches on the boxing team thought it started later than it actually did.

Hembrick and his coaches actually discovered his error about twenty minutes before his fight was scheduled, but the Olympic Village in the sprawling, teeming Korean capital was several miles from the boxing venue.

Desperate attempts to find a bus or taxi failed and Hembrick couldn't reach the gym in time. His opponent was declared a winner by default.)

50

Canada vs. Soviet Union, 1972
When time stood still a moment...

Almost any adult Canadian can tell you exactly what he or she was doing on September 28, 1972 when Paul Henderson scored the winning goal for Canada in an eight-game "hockey summit" series.

It was nighttime in Moscow, but it was still morning or early afternoon in most parts of Canada. For a tenth of a second, our world stood still. Then, as the red light flickered behind the Soviet goalie, Vladislav Tretiak, our hearts exploded with joy.

It was only a hockey game. But it was the hockey game of a lifetime. It was a game that gave all Canadians a sense of national vindication. For the first time, our hockey heroes, our best professionals had been matched against the powerful Soviets in an eight-game series. And our players had beaten them!

Mind you, it was close. If Henderson hadn't shoved that puck under Tretiak at 19:26 of the final period of the final game, the series would have ended in a draw — three victories and two ties for each team. And the Soviets would have been able to claim victory on the goal production, having outscored Canada 27 to 26 in the first seven games.

Perhaps a little historical data is necessary to illustrate just why this win was so important to Canadians.

It had been a couple of decades of frustration for Canadian hockey teams in international play. Canada's first world hockey champions were the Winnipeg Falcons in 1920 at the Olympic Games in Antwerp. But, since 1952, when the Edmonton Mercurys won the gold at the 1952 Games in Oslo, Canada has not won an Olympic hockey title. Even more humiliating is our record of those annual tournaments that the Europeans of the International Ice Hockey Federation are pleased to call the "world championships." Our pride was damaged almost irreparably when the Soviets whipped the Toronto Lyndhursts 7-2 in Stockholm in 1954. Thereafter, Canada gained a modicum of respectability when the Penticton Vees won the World Tournament in 1955 in West Germany. The Whitby Dunlops won at Oslo in 1958; the Belleville McFarlands won at Prague in 1959; and the Trail Smoke-Eaters were champs at Geneva in 1961. But, since then, we had been blanked in international play.

Suffice to say then, that with our NHLers finally up against the Soviet National team in 1972, a win was crucial for our hockey pride. When the eighth game of this "summit series" took place, emotions were running high here at home and at the Luzhniki Ice palace in Moscow. Following Team Canada to Moscow for the final four games of the series was a vocal contingent of some 2,700 rabid Canadian fans. Together, they showed the Russian hockey fans how to cheer, often drowning out the 10,000-plus Muscovites in the building.

Right from the start of that all-important eighth game, there was a feeling that all hell was likely to break loose. A pair of referees the Canadians had had difficulty with before, Josef Kompalla and Rudy Bata, were handling the officiating. Early in the game, Canada's Jean-Paul Parise was called for interference. Outraged, he banged his stick on the ice and was then assessed another penalty — a ten-minute misconduct.

Now, Parise had never received a misconduct in his five years of NHL hockey. So, maddened beyond reason, he raised his stick over his head, threatening to decapitate Kompalla with a two-hander. The ashen-faced referee skated to the penalty box and it was announced Parise would be thrown out of the game.

The Canadians in the Ice Palace blew their stacks. While the Canadian fans were chanting "Let's Go Home! Let's Go Home!", Harry Sinden, the Canadian coach, threw first a stool, then a chair onto the ice.

Although it was a riotous evening, the two teams were playing magnificent hockey. The Soviets led 5-3 entering the third period and things looked bleak for Team Canada. But, Phil Esposito scored early in the third to make it 5-4 and give the nation some faint hope. Then, there was an incredibly loud outburst of Canadian braying as Yvan Cournoyer scored a spectacular goal to tie the game 5-5 with just over seven minutes to go.

More turmoil! When Cournoyer shot the puck into the net, the goal-judge failed to flash the red light. He later alibied that the electric switch malfunctioned but his word was suspect. He was Victor Dombrovski, an off-duty Soviet referee who was to become Canada's "bete noir" in future international matches.

With Cournoyer scoring and no red light coming on to signify a goal, there ensued one of the craziest scenes in the history of international sports. Alan Eagelson, the director of the NHL Player's Association and one of Canada's chief international hockey negotiators, leaped up from his box seat on the other side of the arena from where the team benches were located. He said later he was intent on rushing to the end of the rink to remonstrate with the goal-judge.

Whatever his intentions, Eagleson's vault over the railing from his seat was grossly misinterpreted by the uniformed militiamen who ringed the arena at ice-level. (They had been stationed there since the eruption on the Team Canada bench over the Parise incident in the first period.) Eagleson's leap deposited him right on the shoulders of the militiamen and, thoroughly startled, half a dozen of them seized him. They were far from gentle in their efforts to restrain him and Eagleson began bellowing for assistance as he struggled with his captors.

Out on the ice, the Canadian players quickly became aware of Eagleson's plight. With towering Pete Mahovlich leading the way, they swarmed across the ice, their sticks raised menacingly. Mahovlich led the charge over the boards, and the militiamen pulled back in confusion.

It was a bizarre performance. The players hauled Eagleson over the boards and onto the ice. His glasses had been partially dislodged during the struggle and were dangling from one ear as the players half-dragged, half-carried him across the rink to the Canadian bench. Midway across the ice, Eagleson jabbed the middle finger of one hand in the air in an unmistakeably rude gesture of defiance.

The Soviet spectators, trained from infancy to respect uniformed authority, sat in bewildered silence. They didn't even bother to whistle, which is their form of booing. They were just plain puzzled by the show.

Looking back on it, it seems the Soviet players were "spooked" by the extra-curricular craziness. They too appeared awestruck by all the un-disciplined flouting of authority. In any event, the Soviets suddenly went into an uncharacteristic shell. After Eagleson's ice-dance and the Cana-dian assault on the Moscow militiamen, they never regained their offensive free-wheeling which had been the secret of their success throughout the series.

But, oh, it was still magnificent end-to-end hockey. Many people in the Canadian cheering section and in the media corps were thinking in terms of a tie, and thinking that after all the gut-wrenching ups and downs of that incredible evening, a tied series might have been acceptable.

The members of Team Canada, on the other hand, weren't ready to settle for a tied series.

With less than one minute remaining, the score tied 5-5, Sinden decided to make a line change. Dennis Hull, playing on a line with Jean Ratelle, skated over to Sinden and said, "Harry, you don't really want me out there at a time like this." Sinden agreed and decided to go with the line of Bobby Clarke, Paul Henderson and Ron Ellis. But, fortunately for Canada's hockey history, Esposito refused to come to the bench for the final minute!

The action was so intense in those final seconds that normally it would be a blur and difficult to recall the actual sequence of events. But, so explosive was the climax, that, for Canadians, the images of the final seconds are pretty much indelibly burned into our memories.

Henderson comes down the left wing at full throttle. He shoots from the rim of the face-off circle, and Tretiak makes the stop, but the rebound gets away.

Henderson's momentum sends him for a tumble at the corner of the net. He crashes into the backboards but jumps up immediately and heads for the front of the net.

Inexplicably, none of the three Soviet players near the puck is able to clear it. Esposito, trailing the play, grabs the loose puck far on the left wing boards and fires it at the net while four Soviet players are lunging at him. Tretiak stops the shot, but again, cannot smother the rebound.

Henderson, coming from behind the net and crossing in front from left to right, raps the puck toward the goal at point-blank range. Tretiak stops the first, but Henderson quickly jams the rebound past the sprawling goalie and into the back of the net.

GOAL!

Do you remember how you felt?

51

Henderson's Goal
Reactions

Henderson's historic goal ignited an eruption of joy from the Canadians in the Luzhniki Ice Palace that night and from millions more watching at home.

In Moscow, as they played "O Canada," the music was drowned out by the singing of 2,700 Canadians. Only in wartime could you have heard our national anthem bellowed with such unbridled emotion.

And the story was the same at home. Students watching in schools, classes suspended for the afternoon, went crazy. In offices and businesses across the country, co-workers and strangers thumped each other on the back and unabashedly bawled "O Canada." On the roads, drivers, many of whom had pulled over to listen to the final minutes, honked their horns in celebration.

In cities across the country, Canadians had experienced the moment in different ways.

In Halifax, May Fraser was so nervous she couldn't watch, so she went to bed and prayed. She watched a replay and said, "Why doesn't the Prime Minister give Phil Esposito a knighthood or whatever we have in Canada?"

In Ottawa, hundreds of people surrounded the Soviet Embassy, shouting, "Esposito for Prime Minister!" Eventually, Soviet Embassy personnel emerged and shook hands with some of the Canadian fans, congratulating them on Team Canada's win.

In Sudbury, hundreds of miners and smelter workers stayed away from work at INCO and Falconbridge. "Nope," said one miner, "We're not on strike, we're on sick leave. The sickness is hockey fever!"

In Calgary, shoppers in a large department store lugged easy chairs from the furniture display section over to the TV and Stereo display to watch the final minutes.

The emotion of the moment even reached stately Stratford, Ontario where Shakespeare is sacrosanct and the theatre credo is, "The play's the thing." During the pivotal storm scene in "King Lear," the veteran Canadian actor, William Hutt, ended a monologue by announcing the final score. Pandemonium erupted among the 2,000 high school students in the Festival Theatre that day. "And to top it off," recalls an employee, "They didn't even turn off the thunder."

52

Bobby Orr
Redefining the Defenceman

This man's entry to and subsequent domination of the hockey world reads like a fairy tale. So why not begin it like one.

Once upon a time back about 1960, there was a young prince growing up in a small kingdom known as Parry Sound, on the shores of Georgian Bay, in the heart of Ontario's "cottage country." While he was only twelve, he was such a good hockey player for his age that he joined a team of 14-year-olds from the area and travelled to a nearby town called Gananoque, near Kingston, for a tournament. In the audience at that tournament were a couple of messengers from a large and powerful kingdom called Boston. They were looking for a dashing young prince to come and take over as their leader and king. They had been in Gananoque to look at another, much heralded young player, but when the young prince from Parry Sound took to the ice, he so dominated the game that they couldn't take their eyes off him.

So impressed were these messengers that they spent great amounts of gold to woo the young prince to their kingdom. First, though, they told him he'd have to serve an apprenticeship, to gain wisdom and to learn how to wear the important crown that would be his in time.

The messengers worked it out so that their young prince could serve his apprenticeship in a place called Oshawa, not far from his beloved Parry Sound. Three years later, when the young prince was fifteen, he was among the best young players in the apprentice program. By seventeen, he was the best, dazzling everyone with his shot-blocking, anticipation, his swift, powerful skating stride, his pinpoint accuracy when passing and shooting, and perhaps most of all, his peculiar passion for carrying the puck up the ice himself in spectacular rushes, not usually the province of a defenceman.

At eighteen, it was time for the young prince to begin his ascent to the throne in the kingdom of Boston. The year was 1966-67. He arrived with a flourish and soon after they first saw the young prince, saw his skill and poise, the people rejoiced. They knew they had found their new king.

While it has fairy tale touches, the reality is that once Bobby Orr arrived in Boston as an 18-year-old brush-cut kid, hockey was never to be the same.

Before Bobby Orr's arrival, no defenceman had ever scored twenty goals in a season. He did it seven times in seven years. Each year he was named the league's outstanding defenceman. Playing defence, he twice led the entire league in scoring. When Orr came to the Bruins, they were the worst team in the league. Under his leadership they became one of the best, packing in the crowds and winning the Stanley Cup in 1970 and 1972. And it was Orr the fans came to see. Three straight years he was named the league's most valuable player, and twice the playoff MVP.

Time and again he would do seemingly impossible things with the puck, whirling 360 degrees at the blueline and keeping control through his spin, gathering momentum in his own end and carrying the puck through a maze of opponents, batting the puck out of mid-air — as, in a moment that is burned in the memory of so many hockey fans, he did once while diving across the St. Louis goal mouth to win a Stanley Cup. He had everything: speed, size, stamina, skill, savvy. He seemed the perfect hockey machine, except there was nothing mechanical about anything he did.

From the beginning, however, there were signs of the physical flaw that would lead to the end of his career so early. On December 7, 1966, in his first NHL season, Orr sat out the first of eight consecutive games with a knee injury. As the years rolled on, and the list of absences grew, it became evident that he was playing on borrowed time.

In 1972, he missed the now-famous Team Canada series against the Soviets — something that should have been the high point of his career.

Although his knee was not in great shape in 1976, Orr played and distinguished himself in the inaugural Canada Cup. Eventually, the Bruins, in a move of cold business reality, traded him to Chicago. Gallantly, he tried to help the Black Hawks, but didn't last long. In January of 1979, the Bruins, with whom he would be forever identified, retired his number 4, while the fans in Boston Garden, many weeping openly, stood and roared their appreciation of his years on the ice.

At age 31, after putting his own indelible mark on hockey by showing that a defenceman could be a formidable offensive weapon, after re-shaping the game in accordance with his own magnificent skills, the great Bobby Orr left the hockey stage, hobbling as he went. But, he left it a much-enlarged stage for those who followed.

53

Basic Witness
Tail of Woe

It's a tale they'll tell for many a year at the Atlantic City Racetrack, and it's no tall tale…it really happened.

August 26, 1974 was the date. Basic Witness was a six-to-one favorite to win the Longport Handicap stake race when he was led into the starting gate. Jockey Carlos Barrera sat poised in the saddle as the back stall door to the gate closed behind him and Basic Witness.

Moments later, the starting gate opened with a clang and all the horses broke cleanly — all except Basic Witness. He didn't go anywhere. Barrera gave him a kick and a whack, but all the horse would do was paw frantically at the dirt. Only then did the jockey discover why his mount wouldn't move — Basic Witness had his tail stuck in the rear of the gate!

"No one, not even the old-timers, had ever seen anything like it," recalled Sam Boulmetis, the track steward at the time. "At first we thought the horse just refused to race. Then we thought there was a tailing problem. Some horses will rear up in the starting gate, so a helper will stand in back on top of the gate and hold the horse's tail up. This is called tailing and it usually keeps the horse from rearing up.

"We figured that someone was tailing Basic Witness and forgot to let go, but the film didn't show anyone behind the horse. After talking to the starter and the jockey, we determined that somehow he got his tail caught just as they were closing the back stall door of the starting gate."

Because of the mishap, Basic Witness was scratched and all the money wagered on him was refunded.

"It was a hell of a funny sight," said Boulmetis. "Thank goodness he didn't break real hard or he would have lost his tail for sure."

54

Butch Morgan
Poetic Injustice

Butch Morgan coached basketball at a small Catholic college in Rutland, Vermont called College of St. Joseph the Provider. Before a particularly big game his team was playing in December of 1974, he read a poem he hoped would inspire his team to victory. Unfortunately, the verse did just the reverse.

In the locker room before St. Joseph's tangled with its most powerful rival, Castleton State, Coach Morgan tried to psyche up his players with a poem called "Don't Quit." He gave each player a copy of the ode before reading it aloud.

"After I read the poem, I asked each player his response to it," recalled Morgan.

"I took a few extra minutes to make sure each player had a chance to study the poem and talk about it. The gym was jammed and the fans were waiting for us to come out. The ref kept coming into the locker room and telling us to get out on the floor and I kept telling him we weren't done yet. I felt what I was doing in the locker room was more important than what was going to happen out on the court anyway."

The refs found no rhyme or reason in Morgan's muse.

When St. Joseph's came out on the floor, the team was assessed five technical fouls, one for each starter, for delaying the game. Before the clock ticked off a single second, Castleton's Dave Bove shot five free throws and made three of them. They turned out to be crucial points: St. Joseph's lost 79-78.

Despite losing because of the poem, Morgan called the game the "high point" of his coaching career. "I expected my team to be beaten by fifteen to twenty points, yet those kids played a phenomenal game. In all honesty," added Morgan, who now runs a bar in Rutland, "they probably would have won it…with a little decent coaching."

55

Joe Theismann
Quarterbacking, Canada, and CRUNCH

After a stellar career as the quarterback at Notre Dame, Joe Theismann lost in a close vote for the 1970 Heisman Trophy as the most outstanding college football player in the United States. (It was won that year by Jim Plunkett from Stanford.) A couple of months later, Theismann was in for more disappointment.

Sitting and waiting as the NFL draft was under way, Theismann wasn't picked until the fourth round when the Miami Dolphins drafted him. He knew what the problem was: his size.

"At a banquet before the NFL draft, I met Pete Retzlaff, the general manager of the Philadelphia Eagles. Philadelphia was close to my home-town of South River, New Jersey, so I thought, 'Wow, great, the Eagles.' After we shook hands, Retzlaff said, 'How tall are you?' I said, 'Six feet.' He said, 'You look about 5'11"…How much do you weigh?'

'One-seventy-five.'

'You look about one-seventy.' Retzlaff said. Then he walked away and that was all I ever heard from the Eagles."

Theismann was left with the choice of going to Miami as a fourth-round draft pick or accepting an offer from the Toronto Argonauts of the Canadian Football League. The Argos had offered Theismann $50,000 to sign and $50,000 a year for three years.

Miami's first offer was for $17,000 a year.

Theismann talked the Dolphins up considerably in salary money, but ended up haggling with them for weeks over other contractual matters. He became disillusioned, flew to Toronto and signed quickly with the Argos.

His coach at Notre Dame, Ara Parseghan was shocked.

The Dolphins' coach, Don Shula, was outraged.

Theismann wondered what he had done.

"Gone was my Heisman trophy. Gone was the first round of the NFL draft. Gone, in fact, was the NFL. One of the great coaches in the history of the NFL was furious with me. And I wind up playing football on a fairground for a twice-fired coach whose tailor walked the sidelines with him!

"At Notre Dame, you came out of that dark tunnel and into a beautiful stadium with 60,000 people cheering you. At Toronto, the first thing you saw was a ferris wheel in the distance because the stadium was on the Canadian National Exhibition Fairgrounds. There were no Texas Stadiums up there where hockey is king. The ball yard at Regina, Saskatchewan looked like a converted dogtrack.

"The CFL was a classy operation, though, and my three years there were fun. Somehow, the Argos were pretty good. Our coach, Leo Cahill, was, and still is, the number 1 football personality in Canada. A colourful performer, he was hired, fired and re-hired so many times by the Argonauts that his autobiography is titled, 'Good-bye, Leo'."

Theismann recalls quizzically but fondly how Leo Cahill liked three-piece suits and used to have them tailor-made by a guy called Norm Holland. He and Holland were friends and Cahill would invite his tailor down to the sidelines during games.

"I liked Leo. He had one problem, though, as coach. He knew nothing about football, which he proved my first year by alternating me and the former Detroit Lions quarterback, Greg Barton, who had also been lured north. By 'alternating,' I don't mean every other week; it was every other series of plays in a game!

"No matter what happened, if I took the team 99 yards in two plays and we scored, Greg would replace me on the next possession. If he took the team confidently down the field for a score, I'd replace him. It was crazy!"

Theismann voiced his concerns to Leo Cahill, but the coach wouldn't budge from his plan. So, Theismann resorted to another tactic. He took his fellow quarterback to lunch...often.

"All season long, we ate hot dogs and drank milkshakes. By year's end Greg had gained 20 pounds and couldn't move around on the field. With my help, Greg Barton ate his way out of the Canadian Football League.

"So we've got ferris wheels and dogtracks and tailors on the sidelines, and my competition eats himself out of a job. Wild times on the tundra. What a team! We had two Ph.D.'s on the roster. Paul Desjardins, my centre, was a biochemist. My receiver, Mike Eben, was an expert in Germanic languages.

"My first year there, in 1971, we played Calgary in the Grey Cup in Vancouver. With four minutes to play, our defensive back, Dick Thornton makes an interception and brings it to the Calgary six-yard line. Dicky figured he's just won the car that goes with the MVP award. A field goal would tie it and a touchdown would win it for us. Two plays later, we run a sweep with Leon 'X-Ray' McQuay — and he fumbled. We lost the ball and the game, and Thornton was mumbling: 'If I could get my hands on him, I'd kill him. I had those car keys in my hand'."

Theismann broke his leg early in the 1972 season. The Argos only won one game and Cahill was fired. His third year was tainted by a contract dispute with then-Argo general manager, John Barrow. Theismann figured he was worth more than Barrow was offering him to stay, so he left for the NFL.

"The CFL had been fun, but now I wanted Joe Namath's league. Coming so close in the Grey Cup made me hungry for a Super Bowl. When I left Canada, I had my own pinkie ring made with my number 7 on it next to three little — very little — diamonds — three to remind me of Miami's three Super Bowl's and what I had missed."

Theismann was free to hook up with any team that wanted him in the NFL. Miami was set in 1974 with a young Bob Griese playing well. Theismann looked to the Washington Redskins where there were two aging quarterbacks, Billy Kilmer and Sonny Jurgensen.

After four frustrating seasons with George Allen as coach, Theismann finally became the Redskins number one quarterback in 1978 under coach Joe Walton. In twelve seasons in Washington he played 163 consecutive games, won the 1983 league MVP and Pro Bowl MVP, set 8 club records and quarterbacked the Redskins to two Super Bowl wins.

In November of 1985, one of the most horrific and memorable injuries anyone has ever seen ended Theismann's career. It came in front of a huge television audience watching Monday Night Football on ABC.

Theismann had faked a handoff to John Riggins to freeze the Giants' linebackers; he then was to drop back and look to pass. Harry Carson and Lawrence Taylor weren't fooled by the play-action. They came hard at Theismann, Taylor hitting him and then losing his balance and falling on the 36-year-old quarterback's right leg, full-force between the ankle and the knee.

The leg snapped sideways like a toothpick. Even the Giants' players said they were sickened by the sound. Millions of people watching on television across North America were appalled by the sight.

Trying to inject some levity into the moment as he was being carried off on a stretcher, Theismann said to Harry Carson of the Giants, "Don't you go and retire now Harry, 'cause I'm coming back."

Carson said grimly, "Yeah, but not tonight Joe."

Theismann never played another game.

56

Peter Mahovlich
That's FINE with me, coach.

One of the key ingredients to the success the Montreal Canadiens enjoyed in the 1970's was a lanky centre by the name of Peter Mahovlich.

Playing in the shadow of his superstar older brother, Frank, Peter developed into a great one himself. He had five 30-goal-plus seasons with the Canadiens and actually hit the 200 career goal plateau before Frank did (Peter in his 7th NHL season, Frank in his 8th).

But, in addition to being an important player on the great Montreal squads, he was also chief party animal and team clown.

Big Pete had friends everywhere and tried his hardest to make sure none was left out as the Canadiens passed through town. When visiting another city, as self-appointed social director, Mahovlich often led the team outings to the local nightspots. Sometimes those "social outings" didn't end on time and Mahovlich would return to the team hotel after the curfew imposed by coach Scotty Bowman.

Bowman, being a sergeant-major type, waited up for Mahovlich in the hotel lobby one night in Detroit. Having played part of his NHL career in Motown, Mahovlich had plenty of friends there and felt it would have been rude not to spend a little time with all of them. As he rolled in well after the 2 a.m. curfew one morning, Bowman cornered the affable centreman and said: "Do you have any idea how long I've been waiting for you? ... This is gonna cost you 200 bucks."

Mahovlich dutifully dug into his pocket and handed over the cash. Pausing to reflect a moment, he reached again into his pocket and pulled out another wad of money and handed it to Bowman saying: "Scotty, don't miss your beauty sleep tomorrow night... Here's the money now for tomorrow night too. Don't wait up for me 'cause I'll be coming in at four."

57

Joe Garagiola
Broadcast Bloopers

Baseball has been called "The only sport where the team with the ball is on defence."

Once the pitcher throws the ball, who knows what will happen? If the batter misses it, will the catcher catch it? If the batter hits it, will it be caught? If it's caught, will the fielder make a good throw? Will the runner miss the base and be declared out? The possibilities go on and on.

With such unpredictability in the game, baseball broadcasters have to have a certain amount of spontaneity. Sometimes, that spontaneity can lead to "broadcast bloopers."

Think what the Brooklyn Dodger fans must have felt about Joe Garagiola when he redefined them one day. Garagiola was describing how well the Dodgers right fielder, Carl Furillo, was able to play all the caroms and angles in Ebbets Field.

"He plays out there as if he built the wall himself. He sure knows every CROOK AND NANNY out there."

Even Garagiola's long-time partner, the usually smooth Vin Scully, has his moments.

Broadcasting a Blue Jays game for NBC television from Exhibition Stadium, Scully's opening welcomed fans to TORONTO, calling it "THIS BEAUTIFUL CITY ON THE SHORES OF LAKE HURON..."

Scully will probably never try again, however, to get his tongue around a phrase he tried once on a broadcast. On a ball hit hard to right field, Scully wanted to say, "There's a HOT SHOT HIT TO RIGHT," but it didn't quite come out that way. He quickly learned that you don't say shot and hit in the same sentence if you have to say it quickly.

New York Mets' announcer, Ralph Kiner, once told his audience the broadcast was experiencing "AUDIO TECHNICALITIES."

The Padres' announcer, Jerry Coleman, once had this unique station break: "WE NOW PAUSE TEN STATIONS FOR THIS ONE MINUTE IDENTIFICATION."

Tony Kubek once gave viewers of a game in the College World Series this inside information: "One of the ways to get extra time for your bullpen to get ready is to FAKE A LEGITIMATE INJURY."

Yankees broadcaster, Phil Rizutto told his listeners about a letter he received from a woman who listened faithfully to every Yankee game on her Walkman each night before going to bed. Rizutto's response didn't quite come out the way he wanted, though, when he said, "I CAN'T THINK OF A BETTER WAY TO GO TO SLEEP THAN LISTENING TO YANKEES BASEBALL."

Broadcasters in other sports fall victim to the "word demons" from time to time as well.

Jim Hart, the former St. Louis quarterback, now a broadcaster, joined the blooper club early when he said the Cardinals defence "MUST GIVE THE OFFENCE BETTER FIELD CONDITION."

Larry King, doing analysis for the Dolphins' games, once pointed out that the "DRUG AND BUGLE CORPS WAS ON THE FIELD."

Sometimes, you say what you want to say, but it doesn't sound the way you intended. While doing commentary on a cycling race, former Olympic speedskater and cyclist, Eric Heiden pointed out that the lead cyclist cuts the air friction for the riders following. He described the effect in this way: "THE GUY IN FRONT WILL BE BREAKING A LOT OF WIND FOR WHOEVER IS SECOND."

Best of the lot, though, has to have been from Byrum Saam, a baseball broadcaster for 50 years. He called this unusual play involving the Philadelphia Athletics outfielder, Bob Johnson:

"THERE GOES A LONG FLY TO LEFT, HE'S GOING BACK ... BACK ... HIS HEAD HITS THE WALL. IT BOUNCES OFF, HE REACHES DOWN, PICKS IT

UP, THROWS IT TO SECOND BASE."

No place in baseball for that outfielder ... it's definitely a game in which you have to be able to keep your head.

58

Boris Onishenko
Touché

Spectators and competitors at the 1976 Montreal summer Olympics were primed for the modern pentathalon, one of the most demanding events, where men have to excel at five different sports, including fencing.

A fierce competition was shaping up. The British had a strong team, and the Soviets had sent their best — Boris Onishenko, an army major and winner of the world championship and three Olympic gold medals. He was the favorite for the individual gold medal in the pentathalon.

During the fencing, Onishenko faced British army sergeant, Adrian Parker. Both fencers were attached by electrical wires to an electronic judging centre. Buzzers went off whenever one or the other man scored a "hit." Suddenly, the buzzer sounded. It hadn't looked as if Onishenko had touched his opponent. Still, the judging centre couldn't lie and Onishenko was given a point. At Parker's request, the judges checked the scoring equipment but found no problems.

Later, Onishenko and his arch-rival, Jim Fox of Britain were getting ready for a match when suddenly, the Soviet's sword registered another hit on the electronic scoreboard. He was nowhere near his opponent.

Onishenko rushed off, saying he needed another sword, but Fox asked the judges to examine the sword Onishenko was holding.

What they found was astonishing.

The sword was rigged so that Onishenko could make the judging centre light up even when he hadn't scored. But, on this occasion, it had malfunctioned and Onishenko, the three-time gold medalist, was caught cheating.

Once hailed as a great champion, Onishenko was expelled from the Olympics and disgraced.

59

Ken Dryden
But who's winning the game?

On November 15, 1976 more than sixteen thousand people watched the Montreal Canadiens beat the St. Louis Blues 4-2 in a game at the Montreal Forum. But there was a different atmosphere in the Forum that night. It was as if the crowd was watching with vacant eyes, their minds committed somewhere else. A near miss, a save, a goal, the kind of event normally anticipated and then climaxed with a loud Forum roar brought a muted and delayed reaction, and sometimes nothing at all. At first, we tried to ignore it, but as the crowd's distraction became our own, the game bogged down. Late in the first period, the message board flashed an important score from outside the Forum — "Lib 8...PQ 7" — but there was little crowd reaction. Some minutes later, at a stoppage of play in the second period, the message board flashed again, slowly, each letter bouncing from the right side of the board to the left, one space at a time, in French and in English, so that before the message was complete, the puck was dropped and the game had begun again. I glanced back and forth between the game and the message board, until the board finally flashed to a stop — "PQ 15...Lib 9." The rumble that had accompanied the first movement of letters turned to a silence deep and disturbing. Something was happening and we were all beginning to know it. Liberal supporters, too afraid to think of what that might be, sat silent. Parti Quebecois supporters, also silent, were too afraid to hope. Later in that period, there was one more message — "PQ 33...Lib 15." This time, the crowd reacted, not in large numbers, but like fans in another team's rink, with a loud spirited roar.

In the dressing room between periods, we sat quietly at first, then hoping and pretending nothing was as serious as it seemed; and the one-liners began in earnest; nothing very funny, but we all laughed long and hard.

There were references to "Jean-Pierre Mahovlich" and "...thanks for everything Kenny, but it's all yours now Laroque."

In the middle of the third period, the message board flashed again — "Un Nouveau Gouvernement." No longer afraid to hope, thousands stood up and cheered and the Forum organist played the PQ anthem. And when those Montreal hockey fans stood and cheered, thousands of other Montreal hockey fans in the same building, who had always stood and cheered with their neighbors, stayed seated and did not cheer. At that moment, people who had sat together for years in the tight community of season-ticket holders learned something about each other that they had not known before. The last few minutes of the game were very difficult. The mood in the Forum had changed as had the face of Quebec politics and the emotions surrounding Canada's duality.

60

Gilles Villeneuve
A Matter of Time

"Gilles was always wanting to prove himself, for every lap. I never knew him to say 'I will take it easy now.' It was always the maximum."

— Jody Sheckter, Ferrari Racing
Team member and 1979 World Driving Champion

Gilles Villeneuve was passionate about speed. From the time he was a

boy, fiddling with cars as he grew up in rural Quebec, he chose to tread `
regularly the line between excitement and danger.

Starting with battered old pick-ups before he was old enough to drive, graduating to the famous scarlet Ferrari in which he was killed, Gilles Villeneuve was always pushing himself and his equipment to the limit.

At one point, Villeneuve appeared headed for a sedate life in the Church. He went to study in the late 1950's at the Roman Catholic seminary in Joliette, 25 km from his family's home in Berthierville. He studied classical music, playing the trumpet in the seminary's marching band, and experimented with some improvisational jazz music as well. He admits being bored, though, and was growing ever more fond of playing with cars, driving them as fast as they would go.

He was often caught by the local police, with whom he was a favorite.

"We'd catch him doing 80 in a 30 mph zone" recalls local Constable Claude Page. "He would never argue. In fact, he was always polite, paid the fine immediately and told us the urge to drive fast was stronger than he was."

While Villeneuve was honing his own driving skills, he was fascinated by magazine stories of the exploits of A.J. Foyt and Roger Ward on the NASCAR circuit and of Jimmy Clark and Chris Amon hanging on to their exotic Lotuses and Ferraris on the Formula One tracks of Europe.

By 1970, a 20-year-old Gilles Villeneuve had married his girlfriend of several years, Joann, and was racing snowmobiles with great success. Firmly in the grip of racing fever, he didn't have the money to buy the specialty tools he needed for tinkering with his engines. When his needs went beyond the scope of his rudimentary tool kit, his racing passion overruled his sense of propriety. He resorted to "borrowing" what he needed from a nearby Canadian Tire store's hardware section, walking out with the tools concealed beneath his jacket. This was completely out of character for an otherwise forthright young man. It was something he would wrestle with in his conscience for many years and, later, he went to great lengths to make amends.

Villeneuve began Formula Atlantic auto racing in 1974. His success in Canada and the U.S. was gradual, but peaked in 1976 when he won a race in Trois-Rivieres, Quebec which included several pillars of the Formula One driving community. He had beaten the eventual 1976 World Driving champ, James Hunt of Britain, Australia's Alan Jones, Italy's Vittorio Brambilla and Frenchman Patrick Tambay.

This eventually led to a surprise invitation to join the McLaren team on the Formula One circuit in 1977, and an impressive 11th in his first F1 race, the British Grand Prix at Silverstone. Then came the wooing by, and eventual defection to, the vaunted Ferrari team in the fall of 1977.

In 1978, his first full season on the Formula One circuit, Villeneuve finished 9th in the final driving standings, with a victory in Montreal. In 1979, he won at Long Beach, at Brands Hatch and at Watkins Glen, finishing second in the standings to Ferrari teammate, Jody Scheckter. In 1980 he was plagued with mechanical problems and accidents, and Villeneuve finished 10th in the world driving standings. Wins at Monaco and in Spain in 1981 saw him 7th in the world that year. During these four very fruitful years on the F1 circuit, Villeneuve grew to command immense respect from his fellow drivers, who saw him as a daring and talented competitor. He also established himself as a favorite among racing fans around the world.

There was probably no Canadian who was as widely known abroad as Villeneuve. In Europe, Brazil, Argentina, South Africa, Japan and elsewhere around the world, he was very big news, for Formula One auto racing is a huge, huge international sport watched by millions. Dubbed "the most spectacular driver of his time," Villeneuve was really a citizen of the world. He lived in Monaco, trained in Italy and performed everywhere. There are still more than 150 Gilles Villeneuve fan clubs in Italy. But because Formula One is not a big sport in North America, Villeneuve's enormous global popularity never flourished here.

In 1981, Villeneuve's earnings were $1.2 million, and he carried a $2.5 million life insurance policy with premiums of $30,000 per month. It was during the height of this success and prosperity that Villeneuve sought to make restitution for the pilfering from Canadian Tire during his lean years. He ordered his business manager to make out a cheque to Canadian Tire for $4,000. Talking Villeneuve out of a direct payback like that, his manager eventually worked out a deal with Canadian Tire whereby the company accepted a series of "ghostwritten" Gilles Villeneuve columns which appeared under the Canadian Tire banner in the Canadian motorsport monthly called "Wheelspin News." The company collected on the publicity of the Villeneuve name, and Villeneuve himself was happy to be able to assuage his guilt about the tools.

Gilles Villeneuve died in 1982, two weeks after a controversial second-place finish behind teammate Didier Pironi at Imola, Italy. Villeneuve was ahead toward the close of the race, Pironi was second and it was obvious to all that there were no other challengers after the Renault driven by René Arnoux had dropped out. There was an unwritten rule on the Ferrari team that, in those situations, the drivers stay in their positions. Villeneuve was ahead when Arnoux dropped out, and by rights was to coast to another Grand Prix victory. But, suddenly, with one lap to go, Pironi shot in front in an aggressive move and took the checkered flag.

Villeneuve was furious and vowed never to speak to Pironi again.

In the two weeks between the Imola incident and the next race at Zolder, Belgium, Villeneuve seethed. He talked about it with his friend and fellow driver, Jody Scheckter. Scheckter recalls trying to calm his former teammate, and worrying about the dangers of Villeneuve's blind rage, pointing out the fact that the sport is dangerous enough without having one's judgement impaired by anger.

Perhaps it was anger that kept Villeneuve out on the track during Saturday qualifying at Zolder, trying to better Pironi's best time. He was signalled by the Ferrari crew to come into the pits, that his tires were such that he would not be able to do a faster lap. As he was finishing the lap before quitting, he roared over the brow of a hill at about 200 kilometres per hour, travelling too fast to make adjustments and avoid the slower-moving March suddenly looming in front of him, driven by F1 veteran Jochen Mass of Belgium.

"I saw Gilles in my mirrors and expected him to pass on the left." said Mass.

"I moved right and couldn't believe it when I saw him virtually on top of me. He clipped my right tire, bounced off the front tire and was launched into the air."

The crash was described as "of aircraft proportions," including several horrific cartwheels, driver, seat and steering wheel becoming separated from the car and flying fifty metres in the air, plowing through two layers of catch-fencing.

Life-saving teams were on the scene in seconds. Mass stopped and ran over, as did Pironi and Arnoux. They turned Mass around and the shaken drivers walked to the pits as the black flag was shown around the circuit.

The disaster was caught by the TV cameras and the replays were shown over and over on the television monitors, its enormity becoming immediately apparent. People burst into tears on viewing it.

The crash occurred at 1:52 p.m.

Gilles Villeneuve was pronounced dead in hospital at 9:12 p.m., Saturday, May 8th.

Journalists and drivers wept openly when the final news came.

The Canadian government diverted an Armed Forces 707 jet from Frankfurt to Brussels airport where the coffin, draped in a Maple Leaf flag, was marched onto the aircraft by six Canadian soldiers.

The body lay in state in Berthierville for two days. An estimated 5,500 people filed past the casket. At the funeral, Prime Minister Trudeau and Quebec Premier René Levesque were in attendance and offered condolences to Villeneuve's parents, his wife and two children.

He is commemorated in Berthierville by a park named after him, a museum and a life-sized statue. In Montreal, the racing circuit known as Ile Notre-Dame was renamed "Le Circuit Gilles Villeneuve". In Zolder, there is a monument to him, and in Fiorano, Italy, site of the Ferrari test track, the main street is now called Via Gilles Villeneuve. At Ferrari, they still get letters addressed to Gilles Villeneuve.

Didier Pironi was genuinely sorry about the controversy at Imola. His home was filled with photos of him and Villeneuve. Three months after

Villeneuve's death, Pironi's own F1 career was ended in a horrific crash at the German Grand Prix. His legs were badly mangled and required thirty-one operations during the following year. His hopes of resuming his racing career ended when he was killed in a power-boat accident in 1987. After his death, his companion, Catherine Goux, gave birth to twin sons. She named them Didier and Gilles.

Villeneuve's daughter, Melanie, still a child when her father died, is now pursuing studies in international law. His son, Jacques, twelve at the time of the crash, has decided to take up a career in auto racing. The family is still very much in the public eye in Europe, and is warmly embraced by the racing community on occasions where Joann and the children appear at Grand Prix events.

61

Lee Trevino
Laughs on the Links

Lee Buck Trevino has been one of the most cheerful and proficient golfers on the pro tour over the last twenty-three years.

His happy-go-lucky style has won him legions of fans and a lot of friends among his fellow golfers.

Born in 1939 in Dallas, Trevino was a grade-school drop-out. He did some greenskeeping and caddying before spending four years in the U.S. Marines, where, he admits, he spent a lot of time playing golf on Okinawa. Turning pro in 1966, Trevino was voted the rookie of the year in 1967. His first victory was in 1968 at the U.S. Open. It was in Rochester, and he became the first player ever to shoot all four rounds of the event under par. In 1970, Trevino was the leading money winner on the tour. The following year, he won the Open for the second time and won five tournaments between April and July. In 1971 and 1972, he also triumphed at the British Open. His most recent win was at the 1985 PGA Championship in Birmingham, Alabama.

In the 1990 golf season, Trevino will be old enough to play on the senior's tour.

Never noted for the gracefulness of his swing, the "Merry Mex" has nevertheless won tournaments, still wins money and, with his cheery demeanor, plenty of friends and admirers along the way.

He is also a master of the one-liner. Here are some of his best.

- On the tee of a 600-yard hole:
  "The only way I could get home in two is if I owned a condominium beside the fairway."

- On how fame can be so fleeting:
  "A woman had me autograph a $5 bill and she told me she would cherish it for the rest of her life. A half-hour later I bought some drinks with a $20 bill and got the same $5 bill back in the change."

- About his bad back:
  "If it's heavier than a 12-ounce can of beer, I won't pick it up."

- On the rough at the British Open:
  "At No. 15, we put down my bag to hunt for a ball. Found the ball, lost the bag."

- On the prospect of playing a shabby course:
  "If the money's there, I'll play on a gravel road."

- On losing to clean-living Johnny Miller at the Tucson Open, the first tournament of the season:
  "The Mormons have it all over us early in the year. Most of us haven't had a chance to dry out from the winter."

- On his caddy:
  "My caddy is so fat, I just look to see where he's standing on the green and then I know the putt will break that way."

- On being hit by lightning at the 1975 Western Open:
  "My whole life flashed before me and I couldn't believe it was that bad."

- On how to avoid being hit by lightning:
  "Walk to the clubhouse holding a one-iron over your head. Not even the Good Lord can hit a one-iron."

- On never quite getting it all together:
  "The Good Lord never gives you everything at the same time. If your drives are on, your short game is off and if your putter is hot, your fairway irons are cold. It's like having a 38-inch bust; you also get fat legs."

- On a philosophical note:
  "There are two things that cannot win — dogs that chase cars and golfers who miss greens."

62

Peter Gzowski
One of the Gang

Peter Gzowski is probably Canada's best-loved radio broadcaster. His avuncular, yet probing style on the national morning program "Morning-side" has won him respect from his peers and from his listeners coast to coast.

He also gained a legion of hockey fans when he decided to join the Edmonton Oilers hockey club for the 1980-81 season, to travel with them and to chronicle that season in a book.

In September of 1980, Gzowski joined the Oilers at their training camp in Jasper, Alberta, wanting desperately to get a sense of what hockey life is like on "the inside."

From outside the sanctum of the team, not much was evident. Each day I would try to read the signs: Who was wearing what colour practice jersey? Who was playing on whose wing? Who, in a desperate attempt to attract attention, was trying to start a fight? But, the coaches, caucussing each night in their private suite to pore over their notes and charts, remained close-mouthed. And the players, intent on their own struggles, were remote. I was having a hard time getting a sense of the team.

On the Wednesday morning of their week in Jasper, I put into effect a scheme I had concocted with Joe Black, an amiable photographer who'd been taking pictures around the NHL for more than a generation, and who was in town as part of a tour of NHL training camps. As instructed by Black, I showed up early for Wednesday morning's practice and sat in the bleachers while he set up his lights on the ice.

The Oilers' coach, Glen Sather, saw me sitting there.

"What are you doing here so early?" he said.

"I came to get my picture taken" I said. "For my bubblegum card."

"Okay," he said. "Get some equipment on and get ready. You're never going to get to know these guys unless you get right in with them on their terms."

In the dressing room, the trainers issued me clean long underwear, a fresh pair of white socks, a jockstrap.

A couple of rookies asked, "Are you the mayor?"

"A writer," I said.

The garter belt was giving me trouble. The device that holds up stockings in today's NHL is a major advance from the inner tubes of my youth. It is intricate and flimsy enough to have come from Fredrick's of Hollywood. The borrowed elbow pads also presented an unexpected problem. In my day, even the best-equipped players just had elbow pads. Today, there is a right elbow pad and a left one. A teenaged defenceman named Coffey helped me out.

Now came the real crisis, the skates. I had borrowed Vic Hadfield's and, as I bent to pull them on, I couldn't get down. Partly because of the tightly laced hockey pants, but also because of my middle-aged girth. I couldn't bend over to pull the skates on. I thought of the writer, George Plimpton, trying to play football with the Detroit Lions and having trouble pulling the helmet open to get his head in.

Eventually, one of the young players, twenty-year old Jim Crosson, helped me put the skates on and lace them up.

There I sat, leg out-stretched on the bench, while a man younger than two of my children bent over my skates, lacing them up, tying them neatly and tightly at the top, in a reversal of the time-honored, Saturday-morning Canadian scene. Finally I stood up.

I had borrowed big Dave Semenko's sweater. I need his size to accommodate my midriff.

"Twist the arms so the numbers show." said Semenko.

"You really want people to see this?" I asked.

"Any publicity helps," he said.

I was also told about "the look."

The players showed me how to pull the tongue of the skates out and up. "It looks flashy," they said.

Skate-tongues pulled up, sweater numbers twisted, my greying hair brushed neatly into place, I waddled down the hall. A trainer handed me a Sherwood PMP 5030, right handed, slick black with tar tape on the blade. I bent to test its springiness against the floor.

"For Chrissake, don't do that," a trainer snarled.

"Why not?"

"You just don't do that to a professional hockey player's stick."

I remember the hours the players spent working on their sticks, sanding them, shaping them, blasting off the rough edges with a blowtorch, like hunters with weapons on which their lives would depend.

"Sorry," I said.

Hand over hand, I made my way out the gate and joined the line waiting along the boards. A Zamboni was adding a finishing gloss to the ice.

I took a tentative step outward. As well as being tighter, pro skates are sharper than any I had ever worn. I made a turn, moving in what I took to be a graceful curve, leaning my Sherwood across the tops of my shin pads. From the boards came hoots of what might have been appreciation. Players I had not yet spoken to called my name. "Sign him," someone cried. "Help him," cried someone else. The cheers, if they were cheers, mounted. I felt foolish.

Then the photographer summoned me for my pose, and told me how to cradle the puck and look at the camera. I stole a glance at the stands. And up there I saw ... outsiders.

However, gracelessly, however ineptly, I was ON THE ICE, stared at, rather than staring. I felt, for a moment, what the players must feel all the time at training camp, stared at, surveyed, measured, commented on, their every move noted, their every mistake written down, their every characteristic immutably rated from one to nine.

They are like show animals, I thought, always on parade and always separate from their judges. The game they play is the game all of us played, but the game of our lives is the business of theirs, and they are a long, long way from the neighborhood rink.

(Later, in April, after having spent the entire season with the Oiler players, and thrilling with them as they knocked off the Montreal Canadiens in the playoffs, Gzowski got to suit up again, at an optional practice between playoff series.)

Sather had his sons Shanon and Justin out there and gradually some of the Oilers began playing with them. When someone threw a tennis ball out onto the ice, they pulled one net up to centre ice to cut the rink in half and an informal game of shinny was formed.

I was told to join a team comprised of Glenn Anderson, Doug Hicks, Shanon Sather, and, as a very roving centre, Wayne Gretzky. On the other team were Peter Driscoll, Pat Hughes, Dave Semenko, Gary Unger and Justin Sather, with Eddie Mio in goal.

The action swirled back and forth, as I skated in wide arcs around its periphery. The various speeds of the players made organized rushes difficult. Players would suddenly have to swerve to avoid hitting a tottering child or a middle-aged man.

The personnel on the ice changed regularly. Eventually, the Sather kids retired, and other players joined for a while. Finally, out of the dressing room skated, with surprising grace, the Oilers millionaire owner, Peter Pocklington, his beard jutting in the wind. He was greeted with whoops of joy from the players, who immediately started taking fake runs at him.

Once, I almost scored. Gretzky parked himself behind the opposition goal. Anderson bounced him the tennis ball. The Kid, cradled it, faked once and flicked a pass to me in front. I swiped at it, and watched as it zipped wildly past the corner of the gaping net.

It didn't matter. With the greatest player of his time on one side of me and a nine-year old boy on the other, I was transported back to my own boyhood. However awkwardly, I was playing the same game I had played nearly forty years before.

The game of our lives.

63

Tiger Williams
Tax Planning with the Tiger

Dave "Tiger" Williams made his living in the National Hockey League by being a tough guy.

He played a roughhouse brand of hockey and fought all the scrappers around the league as his career took him through Toronto, Vancouver, Detroit, Los Angeles, and finally, Hartford. He set an all-time record in career penalty minutes and was a fan favorite wherever he played. But there is a serious and impressive side to Tiger Williams that most fans may not know. Consider this account of some deft stickhandling off the ice by the Tiger while playing for the Vancouver Canucks in 1981:

I always took my briefcase with me on road trips and sat up front on the team bus. I never thought that by playing cards I could get smart or make a fortune. There's a lot of dead time on the road, and I thought I should spend it wisely. I'd take along all my household bills that needed attention and any business investment that had been proposed to me. I wanted to learn about business. I wanted to know what guys were talking about when they spoke of deferred payments or cap rates and terms like that. But this caused resentment on the team. I found that a bit bewildering, because as I see it, we are going to have a lot of time to spend after we retire from hockey, and I think we all have a duty to try to prepare ourselves the best way we can.

It was strange that I got so much criticism, that so many snide comments were made on account of the briefcase, because in October 1981 the net result of that old briefcase was that I was able to save myself and several of my teammates thousands of dollars.

I was sitting in my kitchen watching the budget speech from Ottawa and suddenly I sat right up in my chair. The finance minister, Alan MacEachen, was announcing the axing of income-averaging annuities as of midnight. These annuities gave athletes and entertainers a way to soften the impact of taxation on incomes that were high but over a short term. Losing this tax write-off was like losing a huge chunk of your savings.

"Holy shit, they're going for our baby!" I shouted to my wife, Brenda.

I went straight to the phone and called a guy I know in the business world and said, "Can you get me an annuity and get it all signed and sealed by midnight?" The guy said he could but wondered whether I had the money. I said, "No, but the bank does." Because of the three-hour time difference between Vancouver and the East I was able to get the business done in time, delaying payment of a big chunk of tax.

I couldn't help feeling satisfied when I thought about the way the guys were always getting on me about the briefcase. Then I thought, "Oh, what the hell," and I started calling around to my teammates.

Some guys said "I'll have to call my lawyer," or "I don't know about this stuff"; one said, "I'll have to call my dad."

I recall saying, "Geez, I don't believe you guys."

Eventually, about eight guys on the team, including the Swedes Thomas Gradin, Lars Molin, Lars Lindgren, Anders Eldebrink, plus Glen Hanlon, took out annuities in time and saved themselves a lot of money.

Interestingly, the only guy who thanked me was Glen Hanlon, who took Brenda and me out for supper.

64

Gerry Sorenson
Love on the Slopes

The Canadian women's downhill ski star, Gerry Sorenson, won a gold
medal at the 1982 World Championships and four World Cup downhill
races in her career. A very self-motivated and self-reliant person, she
never seemed much interested in romance. However, in the winter of
1982, things changed. Gerry was bitten by the love bug from within the
structure of the Canadian team.

Sorenson had always been one of those racers who had little patience
for the laborious drives across Europe from race site to race site. But,
one day following a race, Sorenson insisted to her coach that she wanted
to ride in the cargo van. Coach Currie Chapman was perplexed. The
cargo van was uncomfortable and slow. An eight-hour trip took about
twelve hours. The demand was very out of character for Gerry Sorenson
— but the driver was Brendan Lenihan.

Sorenson had become involved in a relationship with Lenihan, who
was working on the support team as a video man. Virtually everyone
on the team knew about it, except the coach. There's an unwritten rule
that coaches and staffers must resign immediately if they fall in love with
one of the skiers on the team. Sorenson and Lenihan managed to keep
Currie Chapman in the dark until the end of the ski season in 1982, when
Lenihan finally came forward. He resigned his job out of respect for the
team rules. The following season, the relationship carried on but with
Sorenson travelling on the country-hopping World Cup circuit and with
her sweetheart back home in Canada. It affected her performance as she
failed to place in the top three in any World Cup race that season. After
another full summer at home, solidifying the relationship with Lenihan,

Sorenson was able to rebound in 1983-84, her last year on the circuit. She won a World Cup race at Puy Saint Vincent, France, one of the toughest courses of the year.

All ended happily as Sorenson and Lenihan were married after her retirement that year. Now they coach at the Burke Mountain Ski Academy in Vermont.

65

Expos and Blue Jays
Coming Close

It was the best of times and the worst of times. It was October 1981 and the valiant Montreal Expos at last had won the championship of the National League East. Or it was October 1985 and the heroic Toronto Blue Jays at last had won the championship of the American League East. What ecstasy! What rewards for the loyal followers! Ah, but what blows were to follow.

Steely-eyed on foreign turf in the playoffs, the Expos and the Blue Jays each climbed to within one victory of a World Series appearance and then, returning home, were done in by men of modest baseball stature, Rick Monday and Jim Sundberg.

For years the patient fans had waited for these towering moments. In Montreal, beginning in 1969 at cosy little Jarry Park, they had sung songs and drunk foamy toasts to Coco Laboy and John Boccabella and Rusty Staub and Boots Day and Bill Lee and a violinist had strolled down the aisle, not once but many times, to dance on the roof of the Expos' third-base dugout, swooping and sweeping, the bow never still.

And in Toronto the fans had fastened upon a sad-sack assortment of heroes in the early, last-place years beginning in 1977 — Steve Staggs, Alvis Woods, Jesse Jefferson, Joey McLaughlin, Doug Rader, Mickey

Klutts, Dave McKay, Rick Bosetti – all of them, fans and players, joined in the world's worst ballpark, Exhibition Stadium, where the rolling outfield carpet resembled a painting of an ocean's tide and the seats along the first-base side faced centre field instead of the plate.

But finally, in the 1980's, the cellar's woes were swept aside, and first the Expos and then the Blue Jays won division championships and faced Western Division teams for the cherished pennant. The Expos played the Los Angeles Dodgers and the Blue Jays met the Kansas City Royals, and both came home to Canada needing one win in two final games to march into the World Series. In each case, though, the visitors tied the series, forcing a final decisive game.

Fernando Valenzuela, a tubby, wily rookie who peered at the sky as he came through his left-handed motion, pitched for the Dodgers. Ray Burris, a tall, herky-jerky, well-traveled right-hander, was the Expos' choice. Both were in form on the cold grey afternoon of October 19 in cavernous Olympic Stadium, Mayor Jean Drapeau's epic monument to cement.

The Expos scored early. Tim Raines opened with a double, reached third when Valenzuela was late throwing there on Rodney Scott's bunt, and scored as Andre Dawson grounded into a double play.

In the Dodger fifth Rick Monday drove a single, charged to third on Pedro Guerrero's single and jogged in on Valenzuela's roller to second.

The score was unchanged going to the ninth. Burris came out after eight strong innings and Steve Rogers, the Expo ace, who'd won four straight playoff games, retired dangerous Steve Garvey and Ron Cey. He went to 3-and-1 on Monday. Then the Dodger centre-fielder lifted a long fly midway between the 375 and 400-foot signs in right-centre. The ball cleared the wall.

In the Expo ninth, with two out, Gary Carter walked. Larry Parrish walked. The crowd stirred and began a swelling roar. Jerry White stepped in. He had won the third game for the Expos with a three-run homer. The Dodgers brought right-hander Bob Welch from the bullpen. On his first pitch, White grounded to second and the Expos had run out of tomorrows.

The Blue Jays had Doyle Alexander and Dave Stieb ready to pitch the wrap-up games against Kansas City. Doyle had beaten the Yankees a week earlier in the game that clinched the AL East title, but this time the Royals kayoed him. So it was up to Stieb to determine if a World Series was coming to Canada.

A headstrong emotional man, Stieb had pitched two fine games. He won the opener 6-1. He pitched the fourth game, a two-hitter into the seventh inning that became Tom Henke's win when Al Oliver smacked a game-winning double in the ninth.

This time his control did him in, as it had so often before. He trailed 2-1 in the sixth inning, his team very much in the game. But he walked two men and hit another and now he faced the Kansas City catcher, Jim Sundberg, a veteran the Royals had acquired to stabilize a young pitching staff.

Now, the bases full, Sundberg sliced a fly into a strong wind blowing from left field to right. "It was a fastball, a little inside," reconstructed Sundberg, a right-handed hitter. "I inside-outed it."

The right-fielder, Jesse Barfield, drifted towards the foul-pole, waiting to make the catch. The ball kept angling toward the corner. At the last instant it struck the wire top of the blue-padded fence and bounded back along the carpet. The three runners scored. Sundberg got to third. Suddenly it was 5-1 and the Blue Jays, like the Expos four years before, had run out of tomorrows.

66

Lanny McDonald
Rocky Hockey

After starring with the Toronto Maple Leafs for several years, right winger Lanny McDonald was shocked to find out in 1980 he was being traded to the worst team in the National Hockey League, The Colorado Rockies.

It was to be the start of a strange but memorable turn in McDonald's career. The Rockies, based in Denver, were a rag-tag group of journeymen NHLers nobody wanted anymore, minor league veterans trying to stay in the NHL for the bigger paycheque, and some young kids fresh off the farm.

McDonald and his teammates came to call their Denver days "Rocky Hockey."

"If there was a bright spot about being traded to the worst team in hockey, it was playing for the man they called 'Grapes' — Don Cherry. No doubt, he was the coach I most enjoyed playing for. And from the moment I was traded, he did everything he could for my family and me. He let me commute back and forth from Denver to Toronto to be with my wife, Ardell, who was two weeks away from giving birth.

"Playing for the Colorado Rockies could have been a horrible experience, except Don Cherry made sure it wasn't. After leaving Punch Imlach and all the Toronto turmoil behind, Grapes made hockey fun again. All he asked of you was that you give your best. Coaching the Rockies couldn't have been fun for him, considering he had just come from Boston where he coached the Bruins to the Stanley Cup finals. We weren't going to the finals. Heck, we weren't even contending for a playoff spot.

"Grapes was a great motivator. He'd say little things about pride and love for the game that gave you that extra boost to keep going. One game that sticks in my mind was a night when we were losing to the Islanders 4-1 in New York. There was a minute and a half left in the game and Grapes called a time-out.

"He called us over and said, 'Boys, see that team over there? They're nine or ten goals better than us, but we've held them to a 4-1 score. I just want you to know one thing. Drinks are on me after the game.'

"After the game he took us all out for Chinese food."

There were low points to be sure in McDonald's time playing "Rocky Hockey." Playing in a hockey no-man's land meant the owner of the team treated the operation only as a business venture and cut costs wherever possible.

"No matter who else you played for, you got used to being treated in a first-class manner. Luxury hotels, great restaurants, top flight buses, the works. Not so with the Rockies. On most days you didn't know what to expect. Once, on Long Island, our team bus didn't arrive after a morning practice, and cabs were nowhere to be found. The players ended up on the highway outside the Nassau Coliseum, hitch-hiking back to the hotel.

"Another night, in Chicago, we were waiting for our bus to take us to our game against the Blackhawks. We checked the parking lot but there was only a banged-up old school van sitting there. We thought nothing of it and waited for our team bus to arrive. It was starting to get late and we were thinking maybe we should take taxis to the rink. All of a sudden, the driver from the school van comes over and says, 'You guys aren't the Colorado Rockies are you?'

"That's the way we travelled."

McDonald and his teammates also recall some comic relief supplied in Denver by Don Cherry's famous dog, 'Blue.'

"Blue had his own spot inside the dressing room door, and everyone knew to tread carefully when passing Blue's 'throne.' One morning, a

Hartford reporter rushed into the dressing room to get his story. He was in too much of a hurry for Blue's liking, and the dog grabbed the reporter's pant leg and hung on like any good guard dog! We were all yelling for Grapes to come and rescue the guy, but when Grapes came in and surveyed the situation he bellowed, pointing to Blue, 'That's the way I want you guys to play tonight!' He let the point sink in and then said, 'OK Blue, let the guy go.' The reporter didn't stick around for his story."

Just into his third season playing for Colorado, Lanny McDonald was traded to the Calgary Flames. At first, he was hurt and outraged.

"The worst team in the league doesn't want me. I stood in the airport in shock. The guys on the team had already boarded the bus. I wanted a chance to talk to them; I was concerned for those guys. We had been through a lot together. When you're on a losing hockey team that doesn't have a hope in hell of going anywhere, and you're a long way from home, the guys in the dressing room become family, the best friends you've got.

"I went on the bus to explain to the guys I'd been traded. I tried to tell them what a super bunch of guys they'd been. But, how do you tell them how they made life in Denver tolerable? How do you tell Chico Resch how much you'll miss the late night discussions, how his insight was next to none? How do you tell guys like Rob Ramage and Brent Ashton that their time to shine will come?

"I shook hands with everyone and wished them all luck, then left the bus in tears. As I sat alone in the Winnipeg airport watching the team bus pull away without me, I suddenly realized that my hockey equipment was on that bus!

"Rocky hockey had done it to me one more time."

67

Major League Baseball
Still the Grand Old Game?

The flamboyant umpire, Ron Luciano, left baseball in 1980. He spent a short time as a colour commentator on the NBC "Game of the Week," then became an author and raconteur of baseball stories. In 1988, he tried to get back on TV with NBC, but was told he was not needed. One of the reasons given was that the game had changed so much since he left. They felt he might be out of touch. Luciano pondered on this suggestion.

Has baseball changed? No. Baseball never changes. That's part of the beauty of the game. A bat, a ball, three strikes, four balls, three outs, nine innings, bases ninety feet apart and an umpire to make decisions and be yelled at. The game is played almost as it was when Abner Doubleday supposedly invented it at Cooperstown, New York, in 1839 and Phil Niekro made the first pitch.

Baseball changed? Modern baseball is no different at all except for the bat, gloves, uniforms, helmets, ballparks, the field, the strategy, the players – including the influence of the black and Hispanic players – the customs, conditioning methods, the way pitchers are used in games, the pitches they throw, the strike zone, the number of teams, the creation of divisions, number of players on a team, the creation of the designated hitter, the salaries and the agents who negotiate them, free agency, modes of broadcasting, means of transportation, the time it takes to play games, the length of the season, the existence of a playoff system, the behavior of fans at ballparks, and even the construction of the bases. But, other than that....

In the old days, a fan would usually take public transportation to a ball-park, which was usually located in the downtown of a major eastern city, in time to arrive before the afternoon game began. The fan would buy his tickets at a booth in front of the park, usually asking for seats that weren't behind the poles supporting the stadium. Sometimes, the home team would actually participate in an archaic rite known as a "double-header," during which a team owner would actually let fans see two games for the price of one.

Once inside the ballpark, which was really still outside in those days, the fan would see a field covered with actual green grass, the home team dressed in white flannel uniforms with black shoes, the visiting team in gray uniforms and black shoes. The players themselves were as white as the home team's uniforms. The playing field would be asymmetrical, as it had been built to fit among city blocks, so the distance to the left-field fence might be forty or fifty feet less than the distance to the right-field fence. The scoreboard operator, responsible for manually posting the number of runs scored each inning as well as the out-of-town scores, might be seen poking his head out from underneath one of the numbers. The outfield fences were covered with brightly painted advertisements.

Before the game, players with nicknames like "Moose," "Dizzy," "Whitey," and "Peewee" would put on a show for early-arriving fans, playing a bunting game called "pepper," or juggling, or throwing and catching baseballs behind their backs. One thing they never dared do was to speak to a player from the other team, because of baseball's strict rules against fraternization.

When the game started, the eight position players who started every game would take the field. The starting pitcher, who was actually expected to be able to pitch nine innings (COUNT 'EM, NINE!), would rely on a good fastball and curve and, if he could get away with it, maybe a dab of petroleum jelly on the baseball. Out in the bullpen, wily veteran pitchers who had failed as starters, or young pitchers waiting for an opportunity to prove themselves, would stay ready in case the starting pitcher, who was expected to pitch nine innings (COUNT 'EM, NINE!), faltered. Some teams actually carried one pitcher whose only job was

138

to go pitch when the starting pitcher failed.

When the home plate umpire, wearing his traditional tie and jacket, called "Play ball," the batter would come to the plate, casually flipping aside one of the two bats he'd been swinging to loosen up. A real power hitter might even be swinging three bats. The batter might be wearing sliding pads beneath his uniform, or even sliding gloves that went to his elbows, but he would not be wearing batting gloves, wristbands, or, at least until the mid-1950's, a batting helmet. After spitting on his hands and maybe rubbing some dirt on them to help grip the bat, he stepped up to the plate. Infielders would start "chattering," shouting phrases of encouragement to the pitcher.

In the dugout, "bench jockeys" would be trying to steal the other team's signals or shouting derisive remarks at opposing players. When the ball was hit in the air, the fielders would actually attempt the death-defying feat of catching it USING TWO HANDS AT THE SAME TIME! At the end of each half-inning each fielder would gracefully sail his glove onto the grass where it would remain untouched while his team was at bat.

Meanwhile, up in the press box, "scribes" would write about "mounds-men" throwing "inshoots," and "outshoots," "benders," or "smoke" to "banjo hitters," who hit "cans o'corn," or "daisy scorchers" to the "orchard," where they would be played by "gardeners." If a "gardener," or outfielder, successfully caught a "can o'corn," or fly ball, he would on occasion keep his "rifle" loose by making a practice throw to home plate. Meanwhile, in radio studios all across the state, broadcasters might be re-creating the game from details transmitted by Western Union ticker – and when the ticker slowed down, the radio listeners would hear the player at bat keep fouling off pitches until the ticker started up again.

In the stands, fans would eat hot dogs, peanuts and Cracker Jacks, occasionally taking a sip from a glass bottle of soda pop, beer or other liquid refreshment they'd carried into the ballpark. They'd usually express displeasure by giving the offender "the old Yazoo." Sometimes, though, empty bottles and fruit would serve as projectiles. All this eating and projectile throwing had to be done quickly though as games usually lasted less than two hours.

Before 1921, fans were obligated to throw foul balls hit into the stands back onto the field, and the umpire put it back into play. But, during a game at New York's Polo Grounds that season, a Giants fan named Reuben Berman shocked the baseball world by catching a foul ball and keeping it. The owners realized that if Berman were permitted to keep his ball the revolution could not be far behind, not to mention the money they would have to spend to replace lost baseballs, so they took Reuben Berman to court.

In perhaps the most significant ruling involving sports fans in America, the court ruled that Reuben Berman could keep his foul ball. Some fans wanted to erect a bronze statue of Reuben outside the Polo Grounds; Giants owners wanted to bronze Reuben himself.

And in those golden days, at the end of the game, the fans peacefully left the ballpark.

The key to enjoying a baseball game today seems to be the guarantee of a good parking spot. The modern baseball fan drives to a modern baseball game in his modern automobile, so modern ballparks have been built in areas where "adequate parking facilities" can be assured. Cities put up ballparks with parking space for thirty thousand cars — then build a single two-lane access road to get there. The multi-purpose stadium — the only purpose of which is to generate as much income as possible for the municipality — is used for everything from rock concerts to tractor pulls.

A day at the ballpark now usually begins at night. The games are now mostly played at night so the fans can arrive at the park refreshed after a full day's work. Unfortunately, that also means driving to the game at precisely the same time everyone else is driving home from work. Instead of purchasing tickets at the gate, many fans buy computer-printed tickets at a "ticket outlet." A "ticket outlet" can be accurately described as "a place having no seats between home and first or home and third."

The field inside the modern ballpark will most often be symmetrical, with the distance to the left-field foul line the same 330 feet as the distance to the right-field foul line. Often the turf will be real artificial grass, which neither grows nor dies and can be painted any colour. A huge tele-

vision screen on the scoreboard has become an entertainment centre —
showing statistics, highlight films, memorable moments, replays, and
the advertisements that used to appear on the fences. In fact, the only
thing the scoreboards don't provide are the inning-by-inning scores from
out of town games and replays of close plays on the field — which can
be seen only by those watching at home on television. The scoreboard
operator has become a "computer engineer," whose job it is to create
"enhanced graphics" for the pleasure of the fans. Why the scoreboard
even orders the fans to "Cheer!" at the appropriate time.

Professional and college football teams, basketball teams, even soccer
teams use beautiful women dressed in skimpy clothing to lead the fans'
cheers. Baseball uses a scoreboard and grown human beings dressed up
to look like distressed animals and insects to lead their fans' cheers.

On the field, the teams are dressed in form-fitting doubleknit uniforms
of every conceivable colour, as well as some that are inconceivable.
Before the game begins, players with great nicknames like "Don" and
"Fred" and "Jack" take batting practice and fraternize with the opposition.

When the game begins, the left-handed or right-handed platoon,
depending on the pitching opposition, takes to the field, except for the
designated hitter in the American League. He is prohibited by the rules
from taking the field. He takes his seat. Of course, many designated
hitters couldn't play the field even before the rules forbade them to do
so. The manager has asked the starting pitcher to try his best to get
through as many as six innings, at which time he can go to his long
reliever or "hold man," who'll try to keep the game close until the short
man or "closer" is ready.

When the umpire, wearing an open-necked, short-sleeved shirt, yells
"Play ball," the batter discards his lead bat, batting doughnut, wind
resistor or whatever device he is warming up with, rubs some pine tar
or some other sticky substance on his bat handle, adjusts his batting
glove, wristbands, pulls his protective helmet with its earflaps a little
lower, and finally steps to the plate. Less preparation goes into dressing for a formal wedding than now goes into a single at-bat.

In the dugout, most players are sitting quietly, although throughout the game many of them will stroll out of the dugout and into the locker room where the game is probably on television. Some may even watch the game on TV for a while.

When a ball is hit in the air, fielders stick up their massive gloves, and any ball within fifteen to twenty feet lands in it. The gloves are so big, in fact, that the only time two hands are needed is to carry the glove back into the dugout after the inning ends.

"Curtain calls" — the player coming out of the dugout to wave and to acknowledge the cheers of the fans — are a recent innovation. Old-timers came out of the dugout to play baseball or to fight. The first recorded "curtain-call" was taken by Dale Long in 1956, when he homered in his eighth consecutive game, but today, for far less impressive feats, some players willingly take more curtain calls than Sir Laurence Olivier.

In the stands, as always, fans are eating hot dogs, peanuts, and Cracker Jacks, as well as popcorn, nachos, kosher corned beef sandwiches, pastrami sandwiches, bratwurst and knockwurst, crabcakes, eggrolls, bagels and cream cheese, ice cream and just about any other food imaginable. They might be washing this all down with beer, wine or soda pop purchased at the ballpark — unless they are sitting in the "alcohol-free" section. That means that alcohol is not served in that area, not that alcohol is served free, as some fans thought when they bought their tickets.

Modern baseball fans participate in the game by singing popular song lyrics, among them the classic, "Nah nah nah nah, nah nah nah nah, hey, hey, hey, goodbye" (when they can remember the words). They'll also hold up bedsheet banners upon which they have drawn the local television station logo and written clever messages like "New Hamburg, Ontario, loves the Blue Jays and CTV." There is also the ever-popular standing up and sitting down quickly in staggered sections around the stadium, as well as cheering when ordered to by the scoreboard. Fortunately, fans have plenty of time to indulge in all this extra-curricular activity while at a game, because the games now take three hours to play.

And, at the end of the game, fans in many cities enjoy the peculiar ritual of celebrating a home team victory by running onto the field and fighting with security people or ripping up the field.

Baseball has changed. In fact, about the only thing that's endured from the old days is the ballpark hot dog. They are just as stale now as they were in those days. Some taste like they've been around since the old days...only now they cost more.

68

Bruce Hood
A Referee's-eye View

For a time, before the practice was cracked down on by the National Hockey League, arena organists used to like to play a few bars of the song, "Three Blind Mice" when an official's call went against the home side.

The veteran NHL referee, Bruce Hood, has seen a lot for a guy who is supposed to be one of the "Three Blind Mice." Hood worked over 1,000 games in the NHL from 1963 to 1984. Here are some of his observations on some of the players he's blown the whistle on.

Jean Beliveau

One word describes Jean Beliveau — class. He had it in every sense of the word. He had dignity and poise and was all business when it came to dealing with officials. If he had a question, he asked it in an intelligent way, and always appeared to accept the answer.

Jean did, however, let it slip one night. Referee Bob Sloan had given another Montreal player a penalty during a game in Toronto and Jean took his glove off and went over to shake Sloan's hand — to show him up and make him look silly. Sloan, rightfully, gave him a misconduct.

The next night I was the referee and Jean came up to me on the ice and said, "When you see Bob Sloan, apologize for me. That was not me. It was out of character and I felt badly afterward."

That was a typical move from a class man. Jean Beliveau was and is my idol.

Bobby Clarke

I don't think any player disliked me as much as Clarke did during his days with the Flyers in the mid-seventies.

He would skate in little circles about fifteen feet away from me, scowling and making remarks about the "goddamned refereeing." Never once, in all my years of officiating, did he confront me face-to-face, but he never stopped yapping with those biting, sarcastic comments either.

He hated all officials, it seemed, even the linesmen.

He'd get on their nerves by standing around the face-off circle, looking around, positioning his teammates, tugging at one elbow pad, then the other, all while the linesman was waiting to drop the puck.

Finally, the linesman would say, "Okay, Clarkie, get your stick in here."

Clarke would retort with something like, "Shut up, the people didn't come here to see you."

Gordie Howe

I was always awed by Howe when he came on the ice. He was a legend, and he acted like it. When he got a penalty he would go to the box without a word, as if it was just another part of his job.

Howe was famous, or infamous for his elbows. I think it was a little exaggerated. Howe was taller than most players, and when he went in along the boards his elbows would naturally be around his opponent's ear level. But, there was no doubt he could use them on purpose if he wanted to and sometimes did.

Once I was with Howe at a hockey fantasy camp in Lake Placid. Hockey fans pay big money to suit up and play with the stars and enjoy some hockey stories. Well, in one of the scrimmages at this camp, one of the "campers" was checking Howe a little too aggressively as big number 9 carried the puck up the ice. The guy was hooking him and whacking at his ankles. Howe glanced back over his shoulder and I knew right then the guy had gone too far. As soon as the player caught up, Howe's famous elbow went out like a flash, and, suddenly, he no longer had a pest on his tail.

I guess if the guy wanted to experience the realism of playing hockey against Gordie Howe...he got his money's worth.

Bobby Hull

Bobby Hull's booming slapshot is legend now, and was a terror to every goaltender he faced. But imagine standing directly in front of Hull just as he was winding up to let one go — and not having any protective equipment on.

It happened to me.

During a game in 1968 at the Montreal Forum, the Canadiens were bringing the puck out of their zone against the Blackhawks. Before they got to their own blue line, Hull intercepted a pass and turned around to blast it at the net.

I had been following the play out of the Montreal end and was right in the path between Hull and the net, about eight feet away. I remember thinking, "If he shoots that puck, it's all over for me."

But, he actually WAITED for me to scramble out of the way, his stick cocked in the air and only then let the shot go!"

I saw him after the game and said, "Thanks." He gave me a wink and a grin. Nothing else was said — he knew what I was talking about.

Paul MacLean

It was one of those nights when I had taken as much as I could. Paul MacLean had been yapping all through the game at just about everything, and he was getting on my nerves.

On one play, he was hooked slightly, not enough for a penalty. Play was still going on, headed back the other way, when he started hollering at me. Well, I got mad, one of the few times I ever did, at least while play was going on. I followed MacLean back out of the zone and up the ice, yapping back at him, and stayed on his case all the way into his own end, and even after play had stopped. I just told him to play the game, that I would be the referee, and that he didn't know what he was talking about. I even followed him to the player's bench. I completely forgot about the game and just let go on MacLean, releasing all my frustrations.

It felt good at the time, but afterwards it bothered me. I knew well that it wasn't fair for me to take out my frustrations on a player.

The following summer, I was heading to Prince Edward Island for Rick Vaive's celebrity golf tournament for charity and I knew Paul made his summer home in Nova Scotia. While there, I made a point of talking to him about it, apologizing for my actions. We ended up having a laugh over it and are now good friends.

Wayne Cashman

I had almost no respect for Wayne Cashman as a hockey player. He was a stick man and always had the lumber up instead of dropping the gloves if somebody wanted to fight him.

He was one of the Big Bad Bruins and played the intimidation role to the hilt. He'd give a guy a shove in the face after the play and then sneer at him, but made sure everyone knew that if you messed with him you messed with all the Bruins. He liked that power and took advantage of it. When a guy was down, Cashman always looked ready to kick him.

At times, he was a hell of a winger and dug a lot of pucks out of the corners for Phil Esposito to drill into the net. But I'm sure he was a lot more effective knowing that the opposing players were worrying as much about him and his teammates as they were about the puck.

His intimidation tactics worked so well on his opponents that he tried them out on referees as well. I slapped the Bruins with a bench penalty once because of Cashman's abuse as I skated by. The Islanders tied it up on the power play and I was in for more abuse. But, with Cashman, I'd give it back to him. He'd say to me, "I'd like to meet you in an alley sometime," and I'd say, "You've never had any guts on the ice — what makes you think you'd have any in the alley?"

Oddly, that usually worked with Cashman. It got to the point where, early in the game, he'd start to lip off and I'd just say, "Don't mess with me tonight." Then he'd know I wasn't in the mood for his bullshit and that if he gave me any he'd get a misconduct faster than he usually would.

Wayne Gretzky

When "The Great One" first came into the NHL, boy was he a complainer!

He seemed to have something to say about every call and moaned and groaned a lot. In Gretzky's early days with the Oilers, John D'Amico, the veteran linesman, finally got so upset with the young superstar that he took him aside and really laid into him, telling him to just play the game and not try to run everything on the ice.

Eventually Gretzky came to realize that he isn't special as far as the officials are concerned. He learned he doesn't get any breaks for his team by whining and has made a turnaround in his attitude.

Is Gretzky the best player I ever saw? It's hard to say, because he isn't as spectacular as many of the superstars before him. I mean he doesn't seem to stand out as much. He can still dominate and control a game, but he often seems to do it without standing out. As far as having the feel for the game, there has been no one better. There have been better skaters, better shooters, and better stickhandlers, but none of them have put it all together like Gretzky has. He does it all, both on and off the ice, and has been a great asset to the sport of hockey.

69

Baseball
Batty Over Bats

In the old days a baseball player might go through an entire season without breaking a bat. Hall of Famer Edd Roush claimed he played eighteen major league seasons without breaking one bat. When Bill Terry hit .401 in 1930, he used two bats the entire season. On the pennant-winning 1950 Phillies, Del Ennis and Andy Seminick shared a bat almost the entire year, hitting 55 homers with it.

Today, it is not unusual for a player to go through six dozen bats a season. Orlando Cepeda, for example, would discard a bat after getting a hit with it, believing that each bat had only one good hit in it.

Why are more bats shattering these days? Bill Terry's bat was made from an ash tree. So are most of today's. Wouldn't it stand to reason then that they should be equally durable? Well, no. It's not because the wood is any weaker, but because there is less wood being used.

In the eternal quest for bat speed, which produces more driving force, modern players use the lightest possible bat with the thinnest handle and the thickest barrel. Players used to use long, heavy bats. Edd Roush's 48-ounce bat was perhaps the heaviest ever. Babe Ruth's were 36 inches long and weighed about 44 ounces. Hammerin' Hank Aaron only used a 35 inch, 33 ounce bat. Today, Claudell Washington's 37 ounce bat is among the heaviest and Tony Gwynn's 31 ouncer is about the smallest.

For some, the size and weight make little difference. Ernie Fazio, a light-hitting Houston infielder once switched from a 33 ounce bat to a 29 ouncer, explaining, "The 29 ounce bat is easier to carry back to the dugout."

Players ordering new bats during the season do so with a set of code numbers, so that each bat they receive will be the desired weight and length and the handle and barrel will be the designed thickness. Theoretically, each bat will feel exactly like the others. Once, Ted Williams returned some bats he'd received, claiming the grip didn't feel right. The bat handles were remeasured: the handles were 5/1000 of an inch thicker than the ones he had been using. Well of course they felt too thick!

For all their care and fussing over the tools of their trade, from time to time hitters get very frustrated with them. Hall of Famer Roger Hornsby once piled up all his bats and set fire to them. This, of course, was a classic demonstration of ash to ashes.

70

Yacht Racing
Keelgate

The America's Cup is the Olympics of 12-metre yacht racing. The event comes around once every three years, and is the culmination of years of preparation, experimentation, training, high emotion and great outlays of money.

In 1983, Canada challenged for the America's Cup for the first time in 102 years with the sleek yacht, *Canada One*.

The Americans were the defending champions, and, in Newport, Rhode Island, in 1983, were racing aboard *Liberty*. As the summer wore on, with yachts from various countries vying for the right to face the Americans in the 7-race final, it became obvious there was one entry with a seemingly magical advantage over the rest.

The Australians had developed a top-secret "winged keel" on the bottom of their vessel, *Australia II*. It improved their manoeuvreability to the point where they were able to snap up the good winds more easily than the others. There was much speculation about what the winged keel looked like, but it was under a huge "security skirt" draped around the boat as it was docked each night in Newport. Everyone was curious, and many of the sailing camps thought that if they knew what it looked like, they could better plan their strategies on how to beat the Aussies. Some even laughingly talked of getting up a secret underwater photography mission.

This talk got more serious and, at one point, two frogmen from a Canadian Navy launch, acting not as Navy men but as private citizens, undertook the mission. As it turned out, they were skilled at underwater stealth and were not noticed, but, as photographers, they were a bust. None of the photos were good enough to reveal anything of the winged keel's design.

Eventually, it came to pass that a couple of people on the periphery of the Canadian camp decided to try their luck as underwater spies. Brook Hamilton, a Montrealer, was part of the Canadian yacht's maintenance staff, and Jimmy Johnston, from Courtenay, B.C., was the official team photographer. Both knew well how to operate underwater, and both knew how to use cameras; Hamilton owned a waterproof one. On the morning of July 23, dressed in wetsuits and flippers, each armed with a camera, they set off to get pictures of the underside of "Australia II."

With some difficulty, they managed to swim past the security guards in the docking area and made it under the security skirt that enshrouded the Australian boat. Startled with what he saw, Hamilton began snapping pictures. The THING attached to the bottom of the Aussie boat looked to the Canadian spies like a jet fighter. The bottom edge of the keel was longer than the top, and the wings were huge, spanning six feet from tip to tip.

While Hamilton was snapping away at the stern with his waterproof camera, Johnston was having trouble at the bow. His camera was not waterproof. He had put it in a plastic bag and was now struggling with it, splashing around quite loudly, eventually loudly enough to alert a security guard. The guard woke up the Australian crew who had been sleeping on a nearby boat. As Johnston made a break for it across open water, he was caught and handcuffed by the guards. Hamilton snuck away and was eventually collected by somebody from the Canadian camp.

Johnston had an initial court appearance, on a charge of trespassing, pleaded not guilty, and the Canadians managed to exercise crisis control for the next couple of days. Apparently, there were no questions about the second spy. "Canada One" was victorious over the Italians in the next day's race and the boat was greeted by a large crowd when it returned to Newport, but no one was interested in the crew's fourth straight win. Rather, they were interested in Jimmy Johnston. He was fast becoming an international celebrity. That evening, the cook aboard one of the Canadian Navy launches in the area sent a cake to the Canadian camp for Johnston. It had a file in it.

Ultimately, after a stormy meeting with the Australians, with lawyers for both sides present, it was agreed that the trespassing charges would be dropped if the pictures were never made use of.

One set of the pictures was developed. Hamilton, preferring to let the whole affair blow over, laid low. Johnston though, revelled in his role as the infamous "Canadian frogman," as the international newspapers took to calling him. He once showed the photos around at a barbeque, lost them for a time to a couple of local girls he met, got them back, showed them to Sports Illustrated, and eventually gave two autographed prints to a friend, who later sold them to Canada's national newspaper, the Globe and Mail.

"Canada One" ended up faltering in the semifinals late that summer, and the America's Cup final series was between the U.S. yacht, *Liberty*, as the defenders, and *Australia II*.

The challengers won.

71

Georgia Lady Bulldogs
Stinkers

When it comes to coaching tactics, Andy Landers' methods are "offensive."

Whenever Landers thinks his team, the Lady Bulldogs from the University of Georgia, is playing putrid defence, he announces a stinker of a decree: his players' practice uniforms go unwashed for weeks until he sees better defence.

Several times since he began coaching at Georgia in 1974, Landers has made his players wear dirty, smelly uniforms. He believes defence is the key to winning, and came up with the "B.O. as M.O." after one particularly frustrating game.

"I told the team, 'Hey, our defence stinks. As long as it stinks, we're going to stink too. Until you start playing defence the way it is meant to be played, we're not going to wash any of your practice stuff.' That got their attention. It's worked ever since!

"When they pull on that rancid uniform every day, they're reminded why they stink so bad. If they don't come out and give me a better effort defensively, they'll just keep smelling badly."

The last time Landers dropped this stink bomb announcement was in 1986. Even though the Lady Bulldogs were 15-1 and second in the nation at the time, Landers was disgusted with their defensive performance. So he banned the washing of their practice uniforms for nearly three weeks. On the advice of the trainer, however, the players' socks were exempt from the laundry ban.

"We've been stinking it up pretty good, in more ways than one,"

Landers told the press after the togs had accumulated two weeks worth of sweat and foul odor. After seeing some improvement during practice, he declared, "If we can play a few games like we've been practicing, we'll throw those babies in the washing machine."

A week later, just when the Environmental Protection Agency should have cited the team for violating the Clean Air Act, the uniforms were sent to the laundry. The players could finally breathe a little easier. They only lost one other game the rest of the year and finished second in the nation with a sweet-smelling record of 30-2.

72

Tommy Lasorda
Sundaes at Swenson's

One of baseball's great characters is Tommy Lasorda. He's not just the manager of the Los Angeles Dodgers; he's one of the game's leading ambassadors. He makes regular appearances on the network TV talk shows, and is a back-slapping buddy to many of Hollywood's biggest stars. He also loves Swenson's ice cream...passionately, and won't be denied his regular evening indulgence. No matter what the circumstance.

It's spring training for the Dodgers, Vero Beach, Florida. It's 10:50 p.m. For Lasorda, that's a significant time. Others on the team might be partaking of stronger stuff at one of the many watering holes along the Atlantic Ocean, but Lasorda is a Swenson's man. He loves his ice cream, and he knows Swenson's closes at 11 p.m.

On this certain night, he's running late. He loads his car full of Dodger cronies, broadcasters and pals in his car and races down to the local Swenson's. They arrive at 10:58 p.m., and some guy is stacking chairs upside down on the tables, and Lasorda is steaming.

"Hey! I want a hot fudge sundae," he yells through the door.

"You'll have to see the boss out back," says the guy stacking chairs.

Now Lasorda walks around behind the building and there's a car parked there and it's moving like there's an earthquake.

"I'm going to see what's going on," Lasorda tells his buddies.

"Better not, Tommy," they tell him. "We're in redneck territory, let's get back to Dodgertown."

Instead, Tommy pulls open the door of this car that's rocking up and down and there, in the front seat, are two Swenson's employees, a male and a female, and they're rather busy.

"Hi Tommy," says the guy, pulling up his pants.

"I want to get four hot fudge sundaes," says Lasorda.

"Help yourself," says the guy, tossing Lasorda the keys to the building.

Lasorda closes the door and the guy resumes his friendship with the lady, and the troupe heads inside for ice cream. Now picture the scene: there's Lasorda making hot fudge sundaes — whipped cream, cherries on top, nuts, the whole thing — and he's mad.

"Can you imagine," says Lasorda, "that guy wouldn't stop what he was doing to serve us?"

73

Shawn O'Sullivan
The Rise and Fall of a Hero

It's a story like one you'd see on a black-and-white movie from the 1940's.

Clean-cut, well-spoken white kid shows great prowess as an amateur boxer, develops a great following at home, turns professional and for a while, things are rosy. He enjoys great celebrity, some profit and a nation of sports fans pins its dreams on him.

Suddenly, through some Machiavellian managerial moves, he is in over his head and his career comes crumbling down. He tries a valiant comeback but is unsuccessful and fades from the spotlight, somewhat bitter about the end of his life in the ring and somewhat frustrated with life afterwards outside it.

If it were a late movie, you might stay up and watch it in hopes of being mildly entertained. For Shawn O'Sullivan, it's one he'd rather not see again. He knows how it ends. He's lived it.

For a period of about two years, between the summer of 1984 and the summer of 1986, the Canadian sports public was madly in love with a boxer — not a muscled, scarred behemoth who spouted boxing bravado like some Sylvester Stallone-created character, but rather, a polite, articulate lad of Irish heritage named Shawn O'Sullivan.

O'Sullivan won a gold medal as an amateur at the World Cup in Montreal in 1981 and, from there, rose to prominence as a silver medalist for Canada in the 1984 Olympics.

Then he turned professional, and through a carefully-orchestrated series of early fights, gained a groundswell of fan support, people believing he could become a world champion in the welterweight division.

O'Sullivan was fifteen years old when he decided to take up boxing competitively. His brother Kevin had purchased a set of weights from the local high school and Shawn began to work out with them. One day his father, Michael, said, "OK ... Let's see how strong you are," and they journeyed to the parking lot to spar. But, to learn the sport more seriously required proper training. Shawn first worked out with punching bags that his father had set up in the garage, which soon gave way to the search for an appropriate gym. The eventual choice was the tiny, ragged facility known as the Cabbagetown Boxing Club at the east end of Toronto's downtown core. (Later, O'Sullivan would come to be known as the "Cabbagetown Kid", and it was widely assumed that he had fought his way out of the blue collar confines of the neighborhood. But, he had no real connection with the area, his roots having been far more suburban, white-bread and clean.)

But, why boxing as a pastime for such a soft-spoken and well-loved youth who did grow up in Toronto's clean and quiet Leaside area?

Most of O'Sullivan's contemporaries were burning off excess energy in more socially accepted sports and hobbies, or were just hanging out and chasing girls as teenaged boys are usually content to do. As a lad, O'Sullivan was not even a boxing fan, didn't follow the sport, had never purchased "Ring" magazine or idolized professional fighters. There was no great anger to be released, no innate desire to hurt people and no economic necessity. So why boxing?

O'Sullivan explains his initial attraction to his vocation in terms at once old-fashioned, appealing and slightly unreal to others his age. It was a desire to spend unshared time with his father.

"Having to share your parents with four other brothers and a twin sister is hard. That was one of the biggest things I liked about boxing was that every time I went I got to ride the subway with my dad all the way down with nobody else. Or if I'd go running, he and I would be together."

O'Sullivan says the time he spent with his father was important because he was able to have a lot of adolescent questions answered: questions about life, girls … everything.

Avidly seeking his father's notice, approval and company, young Shawn basked in Michael O'Sullivan's praise whenever it came.

"If he had told me I did tiddlywinks well, I'd probably be the greatest tiddlywinks player in the world today."

As it was, he excelled immediately at boxing, and to his father's delight, it became his single passion.

With his success as an amateur and move to the pro ranks, Shawn O'Sullivan became a celebrity. There were promotional tours across Canada for his early pro bouts, appearances at charity events, blood-donor clinics and two very cleverly-engineered TV commercials that served to heighten his popularity beyond the sports arena.

The first showed Shawn with his beaming, silent mother, Rita, ex-pounding on the virtues of the Swiss Chalet restaurant chain's inexpensive, hearty fare — just the right place to treat a middle-class family of six children to a rare dinner out. "Every boxer needs a little chicken in him," O'Sullivan joked at the end, smiling and charming. He seemed entirely natural, at ease in front of the camera, just the kind of young

156

man his fans hoped he would be. It was easy for him to pull it off because the O'Sullivans really were the kind of family that would eat at Swiss Chalet.

The second commercial was also based on reality and reinforced the "good-guy" image. It showed Shawn and his father jogging through the Don Valley, as they had done for years. It emphasized Shawn's respect and admiration for his hard-working, bus-driver dad, and chicken as the treat of choice for the frugal. In the final frames of the commercial, Shawn throws an arm around his father's shoulders.

Although a lot of athletes make commercials, the impact of the O'Sullivan spots should not be underestimated. They reached beyond boxing fans, beyond sports fans, to the general public, to those who would be charmed by a fresh-faced, smiling kid. Maybe for the first time in their lives, they would listen to a sports report about a boxer. Maybe they would overcome their revulsion to watch an O'Sullivan fight on TV. Maybe they would buy a ticket to watch an O'Sullivan fight in person. The commercials may have been intended to sell chicken, but O'Sullivan's management people couldn't have written a better commercial advertising their own product.

During one of O'Sullivan's fights in Ottawa, while the arena grew quiet during the first round, a fan yelled "Eat your chicken, Shawn." The crowd laughed and O'Sullivan actually broke into a grin, no doubt confusing his Spanish-speaking Mexican opponent. Later, in another city during a sparring session, a small boy poked his head through the ropes and asked O'Sullivan, "How's your mother?"

Yes, O'Sullivan was marketed masterfully and his image constructed carefully.

But, his handlers did not construct his pro boxing education as meticulously as they did his public-winning image.

Shawn O'Sullivan fought and won eleven times as a pro before June of 1986, when his world suddenly crashed down with one loss. It was to a fighter from Atlantic City named Simon Brown. Taking on someone like Brown was a giant step for O'Sullivan and, as it turned out, too big a step.

Anxious to get his boxer on NBC television, O'Sullivan's manager, Mike Trainer, agreed to Brown as an opponent.

The fight took place in Toronto with 7,000 adoring fans there to see O'Sullivan continue on his march to a world title. The problem was that Simon Brown had been through the gritty battles in the seedy gyms along the U.S. east coast, sparring with tough, hungry fighters, particularly in Atlantic City. O'Sullivan, by contrast, had been babied as far as opponents went. Some had been lively, or experienced, or resilient, but none was a Simon Brown.

Brown battered O'Sullivan badly in the second round and with the Canadian in trouble throughout the third, the referee stopped the fight with seconds remaining in the round.

The official entry reads as a technical knockout scored by Simon Brown over Shawn O'Sullivan at 2:37 of round three.

What it doesn't say is that there is where the cruel reality of professional boxing caught up with Shawn O'Sullivan and the career-builders around him.

After that, there was a nine-month convalescence for a hand injury that needed surgery, then a couple of comeback fights that saw him beat lightly-regarded opponents. Then there was a loss in Las Vegas and the final one in Toronto to his former stablemate from the Cabbagetown Gym, Donovan Boucher.

That was in March of 1988. Immediately after that crushing defeat, O'Sullivan retired.

His record in boxing? Admirable. He won two world amateur titles, an Olympic silver medal, a Commonwealth Games gold medal, and a North American championship. He won 96 of 101 amateur fights and 17 of 20 as a pro.

This is not a boxing story that ends in broken-down poverty. In a relatively short pro career, O'Sullivan is estimated to have earned about $500,000 in fees and endorsements. He has invested well in real estate and has had offers from the business world. Married in the summer of 1989, O'Sullivan and his wife, Veronica, now live comfortably in Toronto.

74

Red Auerbach
No-Nonsense Negotiating

For thirty-five years, Arnold "Red" Auerbach, has been at the helm of the most successful organization in pro sports. The Boston Celtics have won seventeen championships in the National Basketball Association. They have been led, at various times, by players like Cousy, Heinsohn, Russell, Havlicek, and Bird. All have come under the tutelage of Red Auerbach. He's a man whose no-bull style has endeared him to his players, those on opposing teams, his contemporaries in the basketball business, and to many, many basketball fans.

Red Auerbach is a tough negotiator, and has some tough attitudes about the process, about how he views agents and how things are done, "Celtics-style."

You oughta see some of these guys at the bargaining table! As a rule, they all think they're experts the minute they walk into your office, and you can bet your life the first thing they'll be spouting is stats, stats, stats.

It makes you laugh. They haven't seen the kid play more than two or three times, but now they presume they're going to sit down with a professional GM and discuss how good this player is, what he can do for the ballclub and so on. They don't know what the hell they're talking about! They study the statistics and study the amounts of money being paid to players of comparable ability.

So they start off by giving you an amount of money their client is after. "Wait a minute," I tell him. "Where'd you get that figure from?"

"Well," he says, "I understand so-and-so's getting this much and my guy's as good as he is..."

Then, right away I know where his head is at. He knows nothing of the economics of the business. He doesn't know that some teams make money, some teams lose money; some lose money even while selling out their building every night, and they just can't afford to pay what other teams are paying.

And, naturally, he hasn't tried to figure out what his kid's actual contribution will be. I mean BEYOND the stats. Not a word about team chemistry, or performing in the clutch, or producing under pressure. Nothing. Just stats.

Well I've always had a little rule about stats, and all of my players knew it. I never wanted anyone bringing his statistics with him when it came to discussing contracts. I don't believe in them.

They're too vague, far too subject to interpretation and prejudice to be of any use in telling you what you really want to know. So I'd tell my guys, "Your salary depends on what I see with my own two eyes. Until the day comes when your stats can tell me how many points were scored in the clutch versus how many came at garbage time, I don't want to see them."

No Celtic player has ever been paid according to how many points rebounds, steals, assists or any other totals he compiled. Each man gets paid according to how well he does what we've asked him to do. In our system, the guy who sets the pick is as important as the guy who hits the jump shot off that pick. Take players like KC Jones and Satch Sanders, probably the best defensive players we've ever had. There were plenty of nights when their great defence against a Jerry West or an Elgin Baylor, helped us win games. But, Sanders and Jones never had any great totals in the stat sheets. What numbers were they supposed to bring in at contract time?

So, with the statistic nonsense out of the way, we can get down to bargaining. But, here is where the agents like to play games.

Personally, I don't like situations where I say, "Here, I'll give your guy $50,000," and the agent says, "No, we want $500,000," when you both know you're going to settle somewhere in the $250,000 dollar range. I hate all the hassling and arguing. So I usually come in with a figure I'm going to stick to, or one very close to it. If I know a player is worth $300,000, I might come in at $250,000, so I'll have a little leeway if I think it becomes necessary.

I also tell the agents: "Your guy's worth about $250,000, so don't go telling me he's worth $1 million, figuring that might boost my offer to $600,000. It doesn't work that way with me."

As soon as they start trying that stuff I tell them, "Okay, buster, if that's the way you plan to negotiate, I'm going to start off at $50,000 and let you sweat your way up to $300,000, which is what we should have been talking about anyway."

The other great trick they have is coming after you with perks: Little frills and bonuses over and above the basic deal. They'll agree with you on a nice salary; let's say $750,000. Then they'll say, "If my guy decides to go back to college, you pay his tuition." Or pay for his trips back home; whatever it might be.

Or one of their favorites: "We want an extra $10,000 if he makes the all-star team." That one really steams me. "Look," I tell them, "if I pay him $750,000 and he DOESN'T make the all-star team, I've got to be an IDIOT."

They all play that game, nickel-and-diming you to death if they can. No Boston Celtic has any contract perks. Oh, once in a while we get a player in a trade who has perks from a previous contract, but none I've negotiated contain perks. I always tell them: "All I want to know is how much will it cost us to get you to play basketball for the Boston Celtics. We are not in the travel business, the real estate business or the automobile business. We are only in the basketball business. So what will it cost to make you play basketball? That's all we're interested in. Make your own investments, buy your own cars, get your own deals at the bank, buy your own tickets home.

It gets ridiculous. A guy making $1 million in salary, plus another $200,000 in sneakers endorsements, plus whatever he gets from commercials and appearances, is sitting there asking you to give him another $2,000 if he decides he wants to go back to school.

So, the perks are out.

When we've finished a negotiation with one of our players, and he's sitting across from me with his agent, we have a standard conversation that goes something like this:

"You like the contract?"

"It's fine. We're very satisfied."

"Good. I'm satisfied too. What about the length of it? Are you happy with that too?"

"Yes. No problem."

"Great. That means if you have a great season this year, or maybe next year, I'm not going to expect to see you back here asking to renegotiate, right?"

"That's right."

"Good. Because I won't do it. Not even if it costs me my job."

Then I lay it out in even more specific terms.

"Here's the way I see it. If you go out and have an amazing season, and all of a sudden, there are players of lesser ability in the league who are making more than you are, that's my plus. Your plus is that you've got a security blanket of guaranteed money for the life of this contract. If you don't have a good year, you get paid. If you are plagued by pesky injuries, you get paid. If you suffer a permanent injury, you get paid. If you're in an automobile accident, you get paid. Those are your pluses.

So you have all these pluses, and my only plus is that, maybe, if you play really well, I might have a bit of a bargain for a while.

"Now, if we're in agreement on those things, let's sign. If not, we'd better figure out something else, because after this, I'm not talking contract with you until this one ends."

I know of a case where a player signed a long-term deal, went out and had a hell of a season and came back and demanded that management renegotiate the deal. He'd been an all-star player, so the team felt it had to. Another deal was struck, same thing happened again. He had a great season and wanted to renegotiate. The team capitulated again. It happened a third time, and the team said no way would it knuckle under again. So the player said, "Ouch, I just hurt my back." The team felt that for $50,000 or $100,000, they could make him happy so they did.

What would I have done?

I would have had him and his "bad back" in the hospital immediately. Bad back? Let's check it out. And then have the doctors stick him so full of needles he'd think he was a pincushion. That might change his mind in a hurry. And, of course, if they discovered there was nothing wrong with his back, you'd have a pretty good case against him.

I wouldn't accuse him of faking it. I'd just tell him, as I walked away from his bedside, "We want you to STAY in the hospital until you're all better. When you're ready to play, you can put your clothes on."

75

Steve Podborski
A Downhiller and his Dog

Steve Podborski was a brilliant downhill ski racer for Canada in the late seventies and early eighties, winning an Olympic medal at Lake Placid, winning eight World Cup races in Europe, and in 1982 becoming the first non-European to win the overall World Cup downhill title.

He finished in the World Cup medals twenty-five times and, between 1980 and 1984, had more top three finishes than any other racer in the world. Podborski also knew the pain of injury and the frustration of rehabilitation, having shredded his knee three times. The feeling of tearing up a knee at over 100 miles per hour on a European mountain is not something to which many people can relate, but, after he retired in 1984, Podborski, in spite of his steely nerves and tightly-reined emotions, also had to endure a pain with which others can relate.

Ann (Rohmer) and I were living in a rented house in downtown Toronto, but I decided I wanted peace and serenity so I bought a house in Newmarket, north of the city. Another reason for responding to the 'call of the wild' was my dog, Dante. Though he had a loving disposition, he was a Doberman and tended to frighten people just by looking like a member of his breed. He also had a sense of humour and enjoyed scaring people by running close to them or leaning against visitors and looking fierce until they petted him. I thought Dante would flourish in the wide open spaces during my "retreat phase."

I really felt the need to get away from it all after living in a goldfish bowl for so many years. Being in the public eye went with the territory of being a ski racer; now I wanted a private life. Another factor in seeking a lower profile was to downplay the fact that Ann and I were living together. It was easier for my parents, but Mr. and Mrs. Rohmer weren't terribly happy about their daughter living in sin. The impossibility of avoiding close scrutiny in Toronto was demonstrated to us one day when Ann went shopping for some cheese for a small party we were having for a few friends. In the shop the proprietor asked her if she was stocking up for the party she was having tonight. He'd read about it in a local gossip column.

The house up north had about an acre of grass which grew like weeds and took me all day to cut. The basement leaked and I had to get it fixed. Ann had just switched from Global TV's "That's Life" to CTV's "Canada AM" and found the commuting a hassle. We both soon realized we needed to be closer to the action for our careers. With all the scurrying back and forth, our place in the country was more trouble than it was worth. In fact, I lost money because I had to fork over cash to make it saleable. Before we left, I was talking to the guy at the gas station near the house. He said the "city slickers" didn't last as long as he thought we might and we had a good laugh over that.

What I did learn from my brief experience as a homeowner was that I don't need it. I don't like to cut the grass and I don't want to have to fix leaky basements or broken dishwashers. So Ann and I moved all our stuff back to Toronto to a small house that Ann found. It soon became apparent it was too small for Dante, and for me — I was using it as an office. One day I saw an interesting-looking place for rent, a very spacious upper duplex, and decided this was the place for me — we moved in and I still live there. With Ann so busy, poor old Dante was leading a dog's life and we realized he would have to go. Ann found some people who liked him and I took him away on our last trip together to drop him off at his new owners' place north of the city.

I gave them his bowl, collar, and lead, showed them how he could heel and all the tricks I'd taught him using hand signals and commands. He was a good dog. I told them to enjoy him and left. I walked down the driveway to my car and just blew up emotionally. It was one of the saddest days of my life. It didn't matter that Dante had a good home. The people were dog lovers and had lots of room for him to romp. But now he was gone. Our family had always had a dog and Dante had meant so much to me. I knew I could never see him again because if I went to visit him it might confuse him. The depth of my emotion took me by surprise. I drove home bawling my eyes out.

76

Vassili Alexeev
Food is the Fuel

With numerous discoveries and admissions over the past couple of years of drug use among competitive weightlifters, heroes are hard to find in the sport. But, through the 1970's, there was a man who qualified as being a hero ... or at least seemed "larger than life."

The Soviet super-heavyweight, Vassili Alexeev, was not only one of the world's great weightlifters; he also probably had the world's greatest appetite.

He weighed 359 pounds, and every day he downed a 36-egg omelete, six steaks, and 20 pints of beer!

But he could sure lift.

He broke 80 world records and, during the 1972 Munich Olympics, he lifted 1,411 pounds. (That is tantamount to lifting a refrigerator over his head.)

Sadly, Alexeev was not in top form when the Olympics were held in his own country. In Moscow, in 1980, he was competing with a damaged hip tendon, and his countrymen booed him when he failed to win a medal.

In the 1988 Olympics in Seoul, another weightlifting hero emerged.
Tiny Naim Suleymanoglu, lifting in the 132-pound, featherweight division, won the gold medal for Turkey.
While his heritage was Turkish, he had been a citizen of neighboring Bulgaria right up until the Olympics. The sports federations of the two countries worked out a deal, said to include quite a big payment from Turkey to Bulgaria, to allow Suleymanoglu to emigrate and to lift for Turkey in the Olympics.
When he won the gold in Seoul, it sent the people back in Turkey into a frenzy of joy. He was an instant national hero in a country that wins very few Olympic medals.
How exalted was Suleymanoglu's status? Immediately, a park in central Ankara was named for him. And, in Ankara hospitals, more than a dozen newborn babies were named after him.

77

The Skydome
How's the weather where you are?

June 7, 1989. Toronto's majestic new sports stadium, the Skydome, is open ... but is closing.
The much-anticipated, 450-million dollar, multi-purpose stadium, the first in North America with a retractable roof, opened for baseball on Monday, June 5th. The Toronto Blue Jays were playing the Milwaukee Brewers that week. The Monday game was full of much pomp and ceremony, and, as it was a clear night, the Skydome roof was left open.

Same thing Tuesday night.

Wednesday was a different story.

The game began as usual, just after 7:30 p.m. Weather forecasts called for evening thunderstorms, but the skies were not threatening as the game began. The roof was left open.

By 8:00 p.m., a torrential downpour was lashing parts of the city, and the storm was moving southward toward the lakefront and the Skydome, with its roof open and 48,000 baseball fans uncovered.

Someone made the call to the appropriate powers within the Skydome hierarchy, alerted them that they would get wet soon, and the order was given to begin the roof-closing operation.

The closing of the roof takes almost half an hour.

The rain got there first.

By the time the real downpour hit the stadium, the roof was more than half-closed. This left fans in some sections safe and dry while fans in other sections had to scurry for the mezzanine or get soaked.

More comical was the scene on the field.

Because of the direction the roof moved when closing, all the Milwaukee outfielders were dry, as were the infielders.

The pitcher was dry, the roof having closed far enough to cover the mound. The unlucky ones were those in the vicinity of home plate.

Lloyd Moseby of the Blue Jays was at bat, but was standing there in a rainstorm, trying to wipe the rain out of his eyes so he could see the pitch about to be offered. Similarly, the catcher for the Brewers, and the umpire, Ritchie Garcia, were being drenched while all other players on the field were sheltered.

After several moments, Garcia called time and had the grounds crew put a small tarpaulin over the batter's box and home plate, waited for five or six minutes until the roof had completely closed, and resumed the game.

Broadcaster Tony Kubek noted that for a moment Lloyd Moseby looked like the comic-strip character, Joe Btzflk, the poor soul who walks around with rain and a thundercloud over his head all the time.

78

Wayne Gretzky
The Great One

Perhaps there never was a day in hockey's long history more shocking to fans than August 9, 1988, when Wayne Gretzky was traded to the Los Angeles Kings. Because of his stature as virtually a national treasure, Wayne the Wizard had appeared to be as immutable a segment of the Edmonton scene as Jasper Avenue itself. And yet, to the astonishment of millions of fans, the Edmonton owner, Peter Pocklington, sent the game's greatest scorer off to the wilds of Los Angeles. In the words of Paul Coffey, a former teammate and Gretzky's close friend, "You're just a piece of meat."

Though he's gone from Canada, at least once each season there ought to be a mandatory moment of silence for Wayne, a simple bowing of heads before the puck is dropped each autumn. No one in any sport so completely dominated his field in the 1980's; not Jack Nicklaus or Larry Bird or John McEnroe or Martina Navratilova or Reggie Jackson or anybody.

All of us were startled a decade ago that this scrawny blond darting fellow, dominant as Bobby Orr, should come along so soon after Boston's marvellous defenceman was prematurely felled by injured knees. In his rookie season in the NHL, 1979-80, Wayne won the Hart Trophy as the league's most valuable player and the Byng Trophy as the most gentlemanly one. And that was his pattern from then on — magnificent play and a gent. He won the Hart, the most coveted individual award of all, for eight straight seasons, and the scoring championship in his first seven.

And those early years were mere harbingers. He'd first won the Hart as a downy-cheeked boy of nineteen. A couple of years later he stunned eldering fans by scoring ninety-two goals in a 212-point season. The numbers were preposterous, even for the present, helter-skelter, wide-open era. Eons ago, in the time of the immortal Howie Morenz, it was a different game. Morenz was a blur on ice who would wind up behind his net for a rink-length swoop ("He made the 7 on his back look like 777," once groused the great little goaltender, Roy Worters). In 1927-28, Morenz won the NHL scoring championship with thirty-three goals and eighteen assists in the forty-four-game season. And Morenz was miles ahead of everybody that year.

So after Gretzky's 212-point season (it was 1981-82) nothing much Wayne did surprised people. Other players, such as Mike Bossy and Mario Lemieux, would leap into the headlines for this scoring feat or that, but partly they were getting the ink because Wayne had reached a plateau where the extraordinary had become commonplace. What more could be said about him?

For instance, Bossy's laudable feat of scoring fifty goals through nine straight seasons was justifiably acclaimed. Still, by the time Gretzky had played eight NHL seasons his reputation was embellished by so many superlatives that there was scarcely notice of his more than fifty goals in all of them. Unaccustomed injuries took him out of sixteen games in his ninth year (1987-88) and the string was broken.

Who knows when he will wind down? He has said he won't play past thirty, which will take him through the 1990-91 season (he was born January 26, 1961) so he is young enough to retain his enthusiasm for a few seasons more.

When Gretzky passed the five hundred goal mark, he said he didn't think he should be included in the category of "All-time Great Goal Scorers."

"Seven or eight hundred is more like it," he said at the time.

He has now passed the seven hundred mark, and has passed Phil Esposito on the all-time goal scoring list. Before he's through, he will have eclipsed Gordie Howe's mark of 801. (Yes, Gordie took twenty-six seasons to do it, but when Howe played, back-checking was not a meaningless phrase from a foreign tongue.)

Constructed nowhere near Howe's rock-boned lines, Gretzky nonetheless has been surprisingly durable. He missed only eight games in his first eight seasons, and tacked on 101 playoff games. So he's been busy. Blinking and grunting, muscled goons have taken runs at him, but he's an elusive waterbug on the ice who somehow performs his magic without challenging the sideboards the way Bobby Orr used to, bursting through narrow holes.

In the springtime in recent years, while most players are restoring their resources, Gretzky and his Edmonton teammates have been prolonging the grind all the way through May, winning four Stanley Cups and dropping a fifth in the final round (to the Islanders), an added drain on the skinny wizard. Sometimes people forget that. A monument, please. Or at least a moment's silence.

79

Pete Rose
The $4,800 Pigeon

An April 12, 1987 game between the New York Mets and Atlanta Braves provides an odd footnote to the sad story of Pete Rose's downfall in the wake of allegations of gambling.

The Braves were losing the game when one of their players, Dion James, hit a fly ball that should have been a routine out. Instead it hit a pigeon and dropped for a double. No doubt inspired by a sense that the gods were with them, the Braves came back and won the game. Rose is reported to have wagered $4,800 on the Mets in the game — a substantial sum to lose on account of a pigeon.

80

Dave Stieb
Searching for Perfection

"It's ridiculous when you work it out on a dollars-per-pitch basis.
Multiply the thirty-five starting assignments by an average 125 pitches
per game for a total of 4,375 pitches in a season. Divide that number of
pitches into the $1-million salary in the contract and it comes to exactly
$228.57 on the cash register every time I wind up."

Dave Stieb of the Toronto Blue Jays — huge salary...huge talent.

For most of the 1980's Stieb was the Blue Jays' most talented, most
irascible and most frustrated player.

Talented? Undoubtedly. Stieb holds nearly all the club's pitching
records and was, on and off, one of the dominant pitchers in the
American League.

Irascible? One of the worst. He has been unabashedly arrogant and
has made regular, ostentatious displays of his disgust when teammates
made errors or sloppy plays behind him.

Frustrated? Understandably, for two reasons. Stieb has always felt
he deserved more respect around the league and, also, he has three times
come as close as is possible to the pitcher's dream of a no-hitter, one of
those being a perfect game.

On the matter of frustration, Stieb even allowed it to creep into the
title of his 1986 autobiography, "Tomorrow I'll be Perfect."

In the book he describes his resentment about not winning the coveted
Cy Young Award as best pitcher in the American League in 1982.

"Show me a good loser and I'll show you someone who's become good
at losing. So when I get jobbed, as I was following the 1982 season by

the good folks who write about baseball, it is not part of my nature to keep it to myself.

"That was the year that Pete Vukovich of the Milwaukee Brewers won the 'Cy.' I finished fourth in the writers' voting. What strikes me as curious is that 'The Sporting News,' whose pages are filled each week by those same writers, named me American League Pitcher of the Year for 1982.

"The first guy to win the Cy Young Award was Don Newcombe of the Brooklyn Dodgers. Among others who were celebrated are Steve Carlton, Sandy Koufax, Tom Seaver, Jim Palmer, Denny McLain, Whitey Ford, and Bob Gibson. If, in the recital of this partial list, you get the impression that this would be pretty good company to seek out, then we think along similar lines. When I was deprived of it in 1982, you bet I was upset.

"Let's examine the facts. I won 17 and lost 14 that season, with an earned-run average of 3.25. I started thirty-eight games and led the league in completed games (19), innings pitched (288), and shutouts (5). I gave up 271 hits, struck out 141 and walked 75.

"Vukovich won 18 and lost 6 with an ERA of 3.34. He finished nine of thirty starts, had one shutout, gave up 234 hits in his 223 innings, struck out 105 and walked 102.

"Hands down, he had the better win-loss record, but he should have had considering the team he had behind him. The Brewers finished first in the division that year, we finished last. Their everyday lineup was, in a word, awesome: Robin Yount (.331 average, 29 homers), Cecil Cooper (.313, 32 HR), Paul Molitor (.302, 19 HR), Gorman Thomas (.245, 39 HR), Ben Ogilvie (.244, 34 HR), and catcher Ted Simmons (.269, 23 HR).

"We were in the 'building stages.' Our big guns, just finding the range in the majors, were: Willie Upshaw (.267, 21 HR), Jesse Barfield (.246, 18 HR), and Lloyd Moseby (.236, 9 HR).

"To say I was robbed of the Cy Young Award would be mildly overstating the case. Just the same, the terms of the award dictate that it should go to the "best pitcher" in the league. I think even Mr. Young would agree that a winning record isn't what it's all about. After all, while he was setting that unassailable mark of 511 career victories, he also lost a record 313 times."

"Tomorrow I'll be Perfect."

One wonders if Stieb ever knew how apt the title of his book would be in describing his chase for the elusive no-hitter.

On September 24, 1988, Stieb took a no-hitter into the ninth inning against the Indians at Cleveland. He got the first two outs of the inning and then on a 2-strike pitch to Julio Franco, watched in dismay as a routine ground ball hit something on the field and took a sudden bad hop over the shortstop's head and into left field for a hit.

Incredibly, less than a week later, in his next start, his last of the season, on September 30, 1988, it happened to Stieb again. This time, it was at Toronto's Exhibition Stadium against the Orioles. Again taking a no-hitter into the ninth, Stieb again got the first two outs and, with the crowd roaring, he faced Jim Traber, only to have Traber hit a soft fly-ball that dropped in behind the outstretched glove of first-baseman Fred McGriff.

Two no-hitters spoiled in less than a week, both with two out in the ninth and both lost on lucky hits…the baseball gods couldn't be more cruel to Dave Stieb…or could they?

The following April, in his first start of the new season, Stieb tossed a one-hitter to make it three one-hitters in three consecutive starts. Then came the ultimate heartbreaker.

On a sweltering night in August of 1989, with 48,000 fans at Toronto's Skydome thrilling with every pitch, Stieb flirted with not just a no-hitter but a perfect game! Facing and retiring the minimum 27 batters in a nine-inning game is a feat only a handful of pitchers have accomplished throughout baseball history. On this night, not a Yankee player reached first base all night until, with two out in the ninth, Roberto Kelly hit a two-strike pitch into left-centre field.

The man who had been nicknamed "Super Dave" had indeed been super, but, as seems to be his lot in life, ended up being frustrated again.

In his book, Stieb justifies his million dollar-a-year salary saying,

"Sure the money is great. But, on a given night, when I pitch to my capacity and win, I feel that I did what I do better than anyone in the world that day."

Maybe tomorrow, Dave.

81

Ben Johnson
Of gold and glory, steroids and shame

"It is like waiting for a firing squad to shoot. The starter raises his pistol, and tens of thousands of fans fall into an eerie, almost reverent silence. All eyes are fixed on the men poised at the starting blocks. All is still. Each sprinter's mind is fully focused. There can be neither hesitation nor anticipation. The slightest quiver of a muscle can leave the runner stranded behind the field.

The blast comes. Tightly coiled legs buck against the starting blocks with a clatter, thrusting the sprinter into a world all his own. Each motion, from the first chopping, accelerating steps to the long, driving strides through the finish, is a battle between control and panic. The runner's heart pounds, his blood courses, his muscles scream. His pin-spikes stab into the rubber ribbon that stretches to the limit of his endurance — 100 metres of exquisite hell — as he chases an insubstantial number.

On August 30th, 1987, at the marble-stepped Stadio Olympico beside the ancient banks of the Tiber River in Rome, the gun roared for Canada's Ben Johnson. He exploded off the start and carved the astonishing number 9.83 seconds into athletic history. He lowered the world record for the 100 metres by a tenth of a second and left behind all pretenders to the title of the Fastest Man on Earth."

Veteran Canadian sportswriter James Christie wrote that eloquent description of the 100 metres sprint, and the glowing tribute to Ben Johnson's world record of 9.83 seconds.

Now, that description rings hollow: neither Ben Johnson nor his sport deserved Christie's eloquence.

In the weeks and months after that record-shattering run in Rome, Ben Johnson accepted the accolades of the world, and basked in the warmth of hero worship by Canadians. A year after that run in Rome, Ben Johnson again astounded the world and again thrilled Canadians at home with a spectacular gold medal victory at the 1988 Summer Olympics in Seoul, South Korea.

It was a sunny Saturday afternoon in Seoul, still Friday night in North America. As was his custom, Johnson bolted to the early lead over his arch-rival, the American Carl Lewis, and a strong field that included the likes of Britain's Linford Christie and Ray Stewart of Jamaica. But at the 50-metre mark, the point where Johnson's lead traditionally begins to narrow, and where Lewis usually surges, it was Johnson who surged and crossed the finish line ahead of the others, with a decisive enough gap for him to turn toward Lewis on his left and raise an arm in victory. When the time flashed on the scoreboard, it was incredible.

9.79 seconds!

Johnson had not only won convincingly in the most important race in his life, but had lowered his world record time even more! That run in Seoul had Canadians at home leaping up off their couches, exulting. It was indisputable now. Canada's Ben Johnson was the fastest man in the world.

"My congratulations Ben, on behalf of all Canadians. You were just marvellous. There is an explosion of joy here," said Prime Minister Brian Mulroney in a long-distance call to Johnson just after the race.

"The gold is for my mother and for everyone in Canada," said Johnson.

Next was the medal ceremony, where a stoic Johnson accepted his gold medal and stood atop the podium as the Maple Leaf was raised and the Canadian anthem played. A nation fairly glowed with pride at the greatest Olympic victory ever by a Canadian.

Three days later, that nation felt as if it had been kicked in the stomach as it learned Ben Johnson had failed a drug test: traces of anabolic steroids had been found in his system.

While Canadians refused to believe what they were seeing and hearing, the International Olympic Committee disqualified Johnson, took away the gold medal and gave it to Carl Lewis. Johnson, his coach, Charlie Francis, his personal physician, Dr. Jamie Astaphan, all maintained it was a mistake. There was even a suggestion that Ben's sample had been sabotaged, that his water bottle had been spiked, that he had been an unwitting victim.

With his disqualification, Johnson was suspended from international competition for two years. Canada's Minister of Sport, Jean Charest, called Johnson a "disgrace" and said he was "banned for life" from competing for Canada.

Just over a week after the disqualification, Ben Johnson appeared at a news conference in Toronto, and reading from a prepared statement, told the world he "never knowingly took steroids."

A Federal Commission of Inquiry, headed by Ontario Associate Chief Justice Charles Dubin, was convened in January to probe the Ben Johnson affair and to examine the overall use of drugs in amateur sport.

At that inquiry, under oath, the real story emerged. Johnson's coach, Charlie Francis, admitted to having many of his athletes on steroid programs. He was convinced they had to use the performance-enhancing drugs to reach what he called "a level field of play" with athletes from East Bloc nations. Dr. Jamie Astaphan admitted to buying and supplying the steroids and advising the athletes when to go on and off the drug program to avoid detection during testing. Several of Johnson's teammates admitted to giving him injections on occasion, and witnesses told how they expressed concerns to the Canadian Track and Field administrators about steroid use on the team, but their complaints fell on deaf ears.

Finally, Ben Johnson himself came to the witness stand and admitted he had used steroids for years, had used them before his world record run in Rome in 1987, and had lied to everyone in his statement after the Seoul scandal.

Johnson was suitably contrite during his testimony. He said he had wanted to win the gold and felt he had to take the steroids because he knew others were doing so. Across Canada there were mixed reactions to Johnson's admission. Many felt disgusted that their support and adoration had been betrayed. Others felt Ben Johnson was a pawn in a large multi-million dollar business, and that his contrition deserved applause and absolvement. Even the Federal Sports Minister, Jean Charest, who had been so quick to condemn Johnson, softened somewhat, remarking on Johnson's "courage" at the Dubin inquiry, and hinted that the lifetime ban on competing for Canada could be re-examined.

Johnson says he will run again in international competition. But, if he does, he will enter as a fallen hero, not an Olympic champion or a world record holder.

In September of 1989, the governing body in international track and field, the International Amateur Athletic Federation, voted at its annual congress to strip Johnson of his world record won at Rome in 1987. Because of Johnson's admission to the Dubin inquiry that he was on steroids during the time leading up to the World Championships in 1987, the IAAF decided to institute a retroactive penalty.

As a result, there is no longer an entry in the world records of track and field that reads:

100m (men)   1. Ben Johnson (Canada)   9.83   WR

82

Frank Robinson
The Colour Barrier

On April 6, 1987, the Los Angeles Dodgers' general manager, Al Campanis, went on national television and revealed baseball's dirty secret. Asked why there were no black managers or general managers in the major leagues, Campanis told "Nightline" host Ted Koppel it was because blacks "lack the necessities." In other words, blacks were not smart enough to manage in the big leagues, even though there had been a host of white managers over the years who could never have been mistaken for professors.

What blacks themselves had known for decades had at last been acknowledged by a top baseball official. Campanis' view of black capabilities was not isolated. It was so widespread that in the 40 years from the time Jackie Robinson integrated baseball to the start of the 1988 season, a grand total of three blacks had been permitted to manage in the major leagues. They were Frank Robinson, Larry Doby and Maury Wills. During that 40 years, there had been hundreds of managerial changes. No blacks have ever been hired as general managers in the majors.

One of the most common excuses major league teams use when they refuse to hire a black as a manager is, "You don't have the experience." Yet there are dozens of current and former major league managers who never managed a day before they got their jobs. Dick Howser and Lou Pinella managed the Yankees with no managing experience. Yogi Berra, Ted Williams and Lou Boudreau didn't manage in the minors, and neither did Pete Rose, George Bamberger, Joe Torre, Jim Fregosi, Roger Craig, or Bobby Valentine. And, despite the talk about minorities needing to get some managing experience at the minor league level before being considered for a big league job, the facts show there are very, very few members of minorities that are allowed to get that experience they are told they must have. Many clubs just do not hire blacks for managerial positions, even in their farm systems. The Detroit Tigers, for instance, up to the 1987 season, had NEVER hired a black to manage in their minor league organization.

Going into '87 there were 16 professional minor leagues in the United States, with 154 teams contained in those leagues. Only 9 of those 154 teams were managed by blacks or Hispanics, none of which were at the Triple-A level or even the Double-A level.

The situation is disgraceful. Twenty-five per cent of the players in the major leagues are black or Hispanic and only five per cent of the managers in all of pro baseball, minor leagues and majors included, are black. Yet many of baseball's powers-that-be continue to insist there is no bigotry in the game known as "America's national pastime."

In June, 1987, then-baseball commissioner Peter Ueberroth announced he would see that baseball clubs no longer overlooked blacks and other minorities in hiring employees. He put into motion an affirmative-action plan, hired outside consultants to check on it and made each team appoint an executive to be responsible for "making sure that fair and equal opportunity exists."

Some teams are slow in coming around.

First, with all the pressure on to hire black managers, there also seemed to be a reticence in the '87 season to fire anybody, no matter how bad ball clubs were playing. For the first time since 1976, no managers had been fired by mid-June, even though Larry Bowa's San Diego Padres were 30 games under .500. Finally, the Phillies fired John Felske. They could have broken ground and hired from within, promoting a black man, Bill Robinson, who had played for them and was a minor-league hitting instructor in their system. They didn't. They hired former Cubs manager, Lee Elia instead.

In November, 1987, Peter O'Malley of the Dodgers finally hired a black for a high-ranking position. It was Tommy Hawkins, a former basketball player, who got the job as vice president of communications, responsible for publicity, community relations, ticket marketing and promotions. His background? He was a radio announcer. Questions were raised among black baseball veterans. Couldn't O'Malley have found an ex-Dodger to do that job? Earl Robinson is certainly qualified. He was an All-American shortstop at Southern Cal who played four years in the majors in the 1950's and then returned to college for a business degree and a Ph.D. He is now the head of the communications department at an Oakland college.

A full season after the Campanis remark, the commissioner convened the baseball winter meetings in Dallas. There were 78 baseball executives in the room representing 26 major league teams. Frank Robinson was the only black. He was working as the special assistant to the President of the Orioles.

By 1989, there was some light creeping in. A short time into the new season in 1988, the Orioles were doing poorly. They fired Cal Ripken Sr. and named Robinson as field manager. The club still finished the year with a brutal record but Robinson, staying on, had his team at or near the top of the American League east throughout the '89 season.

In fact, 1989 was a great season for blacks in baseball decision-making posts. As the pennant races developed, Robinson's Orioles battled the Toronto Blue Jays for the division pennant. Toronto was being managed by Clarence "Cito" Gaston, who had taken over from Jimy Williams just before the mid-way point of the season. Under Williams, the Jays had won only 12 games, while losing 24. Under Gaston, they were winning over 60 per cent of their games. Al Campanis and the baseball "old-boy network" watched two black managers, fighting for a division title, both being candidates in everyone's mind for Manager of the Year.

People across the sporting world seemed to be shocked by Campanis' sentiments, and he was quickly fired. But all he had done was repeat an idea he had heard expressed in closed meetings for many years. There was a two-fold irony in the fact that Campanis lost his job over the whole thing. First, he was only on the "Nightline" program as a substitute for Don Newcombe, a black man. Second, the reason Campanis was on the show was to honour the memory of Jackie Robinson on the fortieth anniversary of his having integrated baseball.

The strides are being made. The biggest commitment made in the right direction and the most significant appointment came as the 1989 season began. With Ueberroth's departure from the commissioner's office and Bart Giamatti taking over, the vacant National League President's post was filled by a black — Bill White.

Sources

Note: Frequently the anecdotes are a compilation of material adapted from the sources listed below and other material from the author's recollections, etc.

1. Frank G. Menke. *The Encyclopedia of Sports* (Cranbury, NJ: A.S. Barnes & Co., 1974).
2. Stan Fischler. *Amazing Trivia from the World of Baseball* (Toronto: Penguin, 1984).
3. *New York Herald Tribune*, July 25, 1908.
4. Stan Fischler. *Amazing Trivia from the World of Football* (Toronto: Penguin, 1984).
5. Paulette Bourgeois. *On Your Mark, Get Set: All About the Olympics Then & Now* (Toronto: Kidscan Press, 1987).
6. John Durant. *Highlights of the Olympics* (New York: Hastings House, 1969).
7. Jerry Izenberg. *The Rivals* (New York: Holt, Rinehart & Winston, 1962).
8. Larry Bornstein. *After Olympic Glory* (New York: Frederick Warne & Co., 1978).
9. Ronald Reagan and Richard G. Hubler. *Where's the Rest of Me?* (New York: E.P. Dutton, 1965).
10. Stan Fischler. *Amazing Trivia from the World of Hockey* (Toronto: Penguin, 1983).
11. Stan Fischler. *Amazing Trivia from the World of Baseball* (Toronto: Penguin, 1984).
12. Stan Fischler. *Amazing Trivia from the World of Baseball* (Toronto: Penguin, 1984).
13. Yogi Berra with Tom Horton. *Yogi...It Ain't Over* (New York: McGraw-Hill, 1989).
14. Scott Young. *Hello Canada* (Toronto: Seal Books, 1985).
15. Paulette Bourgeois. *On Your Mark, Get Set: All About the Olympics Then & Now* (Toronto: Kidscan Press, 1987).
16. Stan Fischler. *Amazing Trivia from the World of Hockey* (Toronto: Penguin, 1983).

18. Stan Fischler. *Amazing Trivia from the World of Hockey* (Toronto: Penguin, 1983).
19. Paulette Bourgeois. *On Your Mark, Get Set: All About the Olympics Then & Now* (Toronto: Kidscan Press, 1987).
20. Stan Fischler. *Amazing Trivia from the World of Hockey* (Toronto: Penguin, 1983).
21. Edmund Hillary. *High Adventure* (London: Hodder & Stoughton, 1955).
22. Grant Kerr in *Winners: A Century of Canadian Sport* (Toronto: Grosvenor House, 1985).
23. Scott Young. *Gordon Sinclair: A Life...and Then Some* (Toronto: Macmillan of Canada, 1987).
24. Stan Fischler. *Amazing Trivia from the World of Hockey* (Toronto: Penguin, 1983).
25. Bruce Nash and Alan Zullo. *The Sports Hall of Shame* (Toronto: Pocketbooks, 1987).
27. Robert Smith. *The World Series* (Garden City, NJ: Doubleday, 1967).
28. Yogi Berra with Tom Horton. *Yogi...It Ain't Over* (New York: McGraw-Hill, 1989).
29. Stan Fischler. *Those Were the Days* (New York: Dodd Mead, 1976).
30. Sam Snead and George Mendoza. *Slammin' Sam* (General Publishing, 1986).
31. Stan Fischler. *Amazing Trivia from the World of Baseball* (Toronto: Penguin, 1984).
32. *Toronto Star*; Associated Press.
33. Neil Davidson in *Winners: A Century of Canadian Sport* (Toronto: Grosvenor House, 1985).
34. Joe Garagiola. *It's Anybody's Ballgame* (Contemporary Books, 1988).
35. William Houston. *Ballard* (Toronto: Summerhill Press, 1984).
36. Bruce Nash and Alan Zullo. *The Sports Hall of Shame. (Toronto: Pocketbooks, 1987).*
37. Dick Irvin. *Now Back to You Dick* (Toronto: McClelland & Stewart, 1988).
38. Jim Coleman in *Winners: A Century of Canadian Sport* (Grosvenor House, 1985).
39. Stan Fischler. *Amazing Trivia from the World of Football* (Toronto: Penguin, 1984).
40. Alexander Weyand. *Football Immortals* (London: Macmillan, 1962).
41. Jay Johnstone and Rick Talley. *Over the Edge* (Contemporary Books, 1987).
42. Ken Stabler and Berry Stainbeck. *Snake* (New York: Doubleday, 1986).
43. Jim Benagh. *Incredible Olympic Feats* (New York: McGraw-Hill, 1976).
44. Stan Fischler. *Amazing Trivia from the World of Football* (Toronto: Penguin, 1984).
45. Jack Sullivan. *The Grey Cup Story* (Toronto: Greywood Publishing, 1972).
46. Martin O'Malley. *Gross Misconduct* (Toronto: Viking Penguin, 1988).
47. Larry Robinson with Chris Goyens. *Robinson for the Defence* (McGraw-Hill Ryerson, 1988).

48. Bruce Nash and Alan Zullo. *The Sports Hall of Shame*. (Toronto: Pocketbooks, 1987).
49. Paulette Bourgeois. *On Your Mark, Get Set: All About the Olympics Then & Now* (Toronto: Kidscan Press, 1987).
50. Jim Coleman. *Hockey is Our Game* (Toronto: Key Porter, 1987).
51. *Toronto Star*, Sept. 29, 1972.
52. Peter Gzowski. *The Game of Our Lives* (Toronto: McClelland & Stewart, 1981).
53. Bruce Nash and Alan Zullo. *The Sports Hall of Shame*. (Toronto: Pocketbooks, 1987).
54. Bruce Nash and Alan Zullo. *The Sports Hall of Shame*. (Toronto: Pocketbooks, 1987).
55. Joe Theismann and Dave Kindred. *Theismann* (Contemporary Books, 1987).
56. Larry Robinson with Chris Goyens. *Robinson for the Defence* (McGraw-Hill Ryerson, 1988).
57. Joe Garagiola. *It's Anybody's Ballgame* (Contemporary Books, 1988).
58. Paulette Bourgeois. *On Your Mark, Get Set: All About the Olympics Then & Now* (Toronto: Kidscan Press, 1987).
59. Ken Dryden. *The Game* (Toronto: Macmillan of Canada, 1983).
60. Gerald Donaldson. *Gilles Villeneuve: The Life of a Legendary Racing Driver* (Toronto: McClelland and Stewart, 1989) and Guy Robillard in *Winners: A Century Of Canadian Sport* (Toronto: Grosvenor House, 1985).
61. Gary Alan Price. *Hot Air* (Gary Alan Price, 1987).
62. Peter Gzowski. *The Game of Our Lives* (Toronto: McClelland & Stewart, 1981).
63. Dave Williams with James Lawton. *Tiger: A Hockey Story* (Vancouver: Douglas & McIntyre, 1985).
64. Currie Chapman with Randy Starkman. *On the Edge* (Toronto: McGraw-Hill Ryerson, 1988).
65. Trent Frayne. *The Best of Times* (Toronto: Key Porter, 1988).
66. Lanny McDonald with Steve Simmons. *Lanny* (Toronto: McGraw-Hill Ryerson, 1987).
67. Ron Luciano and David Fisher. *Remembrance of Swings Past* (New York: Bantam Books, 1988).
68. Bruce Hood with Murray Townsend. *Calling the Shots* (Toronto: Stoddart, 1988).
69. Ron Luciano and David Fisher. *Remembrance of Swings Past* (New York: Bantam Books, 1988).
70. Jeff Boyd and Doug Hunter. *Trials* (Toronto: Macmillan of Canada, 1984).
71. Bruce Nash and Alan Zullo. *The Sports Hall of Shame*. *(Toronto: Pocketbooks, 1987)*.
72. Jay Johnstone and Rick Talley. *Over the Edge* (Contemporary Books, 1987).
73. Stephen Brunt. *Mean Business: The Creation of Shawn O'Sullivan* (Toronto: Penguin, 1987).
74. Red Auerbach with Joe Fitzgerald. *On and Off the Court* (New York: Macmillan Inc., 1985).

75. Steve Podborski and Gerald Donaldson. *Podborski* (McClelland and Stewart, 1986).
76. Paulette Bourgeois. *On Your Mark, Get Set: All About the Olympics Then & Now* (Toronto: Kidscan Press, 1987).
78. Trent Frayne. *The Best of Times* (Toronto: Key Porter, 1988).
79. Associated Press, July, 1989.
80. Dave Stieb with Kevin Boland. *Tomorrow I'll Be Perfect* (Toronto: Doubleday, 1986).
81. James R. Christie. *Ben Johnson: The Fastest Man on Earth* (Toronto: Seal Books, 1988).
82. Frank Robinson with Berry Stainbeck. *Extra Innings* (New York: McGraw-Hill, 1988).

Index

References are to anecdote numbers.

Plimpton, George 62
Pocklington, Peter 62, 78
Podborski, Steve 75
Preakness, the 38
Prentice, Dean 20
Prince George, B.C. 46
Pulford, Bob 46
Rader, Doug 65
Raines, Tim 65
Ramage, Rob 66
Reagan, Ronald 7, 9
Resch, Chico 66
Richard, Maurice (Rocket) 24
Richardson, Bobby 27, 28
Riggins, John 55
Ripken, Cal 82
Rizutto, Phil 57
Robinson, Frank 82
Robinson, Jackie 82
Robinson, Jeffery 47
Robinson, Larry 47
Robinson, Rey 49
Rockne, Knute 7
Rose, Pete 79, 82
Roush, Eddie 69
rowing 5, 8
rugby 4
Ruth, Babe 6, 69
Ryan, Chuck 25
sailing 70
San Francisco 50ers 39
Saskatchewan Roughriders 45
Sather, Glen 62
Sather, Justin 62
Sawchuk, Terry 20
Scheckter, Jody 60
Scott, Barbara Ann 15
Scully, Vin 57
Segal, Abe 36
Selke, Frank 24
Semenko, Dave 62
Seminick, Andy 69
Seoul Olympics 49
Shakespeare, William 1
Shoemaker, Willie 38

Shore, Eddie 10, 17
Sinclair, Gordon 23
Sinden, Harry 50
skating, figure 15
skating, speed 57
ski jumping 25
skiing 64, 75
Skowron, Moose 27, 28
Skydome 77
Slaughter, Enos 34
Sloan, Bob 68
Smythe, Conn 23, 35
Smythe, Stafford 35
Snead, Sam 30
soccer 1, 40, 48
Sorenson, Gerry 64
speed skating 57
Spencer, Brian 46
Spencer, Roy 46
Spock, Benjamin 8
St. Louis Blues 20, 52, 59
Stabler, Ken 42
Staggs, Steve 65
Stanley Cup 24, 52
Staub, Rusty 65
Stengel, Casey 11
Stewart, Ron 45
Stieb, Dave 65, 80
Stratford Festival 51
Sugar Bowl 42
Suleymanoglu, Naim 76
Sullivan, Jack 33
Sunberg, Jim 65
Taylor, E.P. 38
Taylor, Lawrence 55
tennis 36
Terry, Bill 69
Theisman, Joe 55
Thompson, Cliff 24
Thornton, Dick 55
Thorpe, Jim 6
Toronto Maple Leafs 23
Toronto Star 23
Toronto Argonauts (football) 35, 45, 55
Toronto Argonauts (rowing) 5